I0114262

SILVER SPRINGS

Silver Springs—The Liquid Heart of Florida
Copyright © 2020
Robert L. Knight, Ph.D. and Marian Rizzo

ISBN: 978-1-952474-40-8

Cover art courtesy Florida Archives PC3318

All rights reserved. No part of this book may be reproduced, stored in a retrieval system, or transmitted in any form or by any means—electronic, mechanical, photocopy, recording or otherwise—without the prior written permission of the publisher. The only exception is brief quotations for review purposes.

Published by WordCrafts Press
Cody, Wyoming 82414
www.wordcrafts.net

SILVER SPRINGS
THE LIQUID HEART OF FLORIDA

Its Past, Its Present, and Its Future

Robert L. Knight, Ph.D.
&
Marian Rizzo

WordCrafts Press

Some of the subjects in these stories have passed away.
This book is dedicated to their memory and to the
many folks who enjoy Florida's most precious resource
and are committed to preserving it for future generations.

CONTENTS

PREFACE

Central Florida's Silver Springs is perhaps the best known natural artesian spring in the world. A grand hydrographical feature on par with Niagara Falls and the Mississippian River according to one early traveler in the 1850s. Also, the largest spring in the world based on long-term average measured flows—more than 500 million gallons per day equivalent to the water consumption of 5 million Floridians. Silver Springs is also the most visited spring system in the U.S. (formerly more than one million tourists each year before Disney) and the most studied. In fact, Silver Springs is the "Fountain of Knowledge" about how all aquatic ecosystems function, based on a landmark, holistic, ecosystem study conducted more than 70 years ago.

The authors have been under the influence of this "well-spring of magical elixir" for as long as we can remember. Having visited on family outings as early as the 1950s, conducting graduate research and continuing monitoring in the Silver River, to writing for the *Ocala Star Banner* for more than 30 years, we have experienced the Silver Springs and Silver River above and below water, and know much about the million acre springshed that collects and recharges the rainwater that supplies its lifeblood.

We have undertaken the assembly of this book and these photos through a feeling of responsibility. A diminishing number of Ocala's living residents remember the Silver Springs of Carl Ray and "Shorty" Davidson, the golden years under the management of the American Broadcasting Corporation, the cheesy movies and TV series of the distant past, the swimming beach and floating platform at the Head Spring, and the attempt at cultural equity at Paradise Park. This book weaves together the first-hand recollections of many of the people who made history at Silver Springs with the underlying and more universal plight of the spring during the more recent past. Silver Springs, in many ways the Heart of Florida, is fading due to the careless apathy of the public and the clever manipulations of truth by unscrupulous proponents of poorly regulated growth and development. We believe it is essential to the future of Silver Springs as well as to the future of Florida herself, to educate and activate your civic pride and to invite you to join in the struggle to Save Silver Springs.

Robert L. Knight and Marian Rizzo, 2020

INTRODUCTION TO FLORIDA'S SPRINGS

Robert L. Knight, Ph.D., Director, Howard T. Odum Florida Springs Institute
(This article originally appeared in *Underwater Speleology Magazine*)

Florida is blessed with over 1,000 documented artesian springs. These springs historically discharged over 10 billion gallons per day of groundwater from the Floridan Aquifer System (FAS). The modern springs of Florida are likely no older than the beginning of the Pleistocene Epoch, about 2.6 million years ago when a long series of sea level fluctuations exposed and reflooded the carbonate (limestone) Florida Platform. Following the last Ice Age, early humans in Florida left artifacts and cut marks on bones of extinct megafauna in sinkholes and caves, including inside Mammoth Cave—30 feet below the current water surface at Silver Springs. Clearly, groundwater levels were much lower when these karst features were occupied by humans and the megafauna they hunted.

Most of those formerly dry caves are today's springs, illustrating how aquifer levels and spring flows drastically change over geologic time. In the Holocene Epoch (last 12,000 years) ample and consistent rainfall returned to Florida, displacing saltwater and refilling the limestone aquifer with an abundance of freshwater. As aquifer levels rose above the edges of the existing sinkholes, they took life

(Photo: Florida Archives)

Scuba divers at the entrance to Mammoth Cave, the largest spring feeding groundwater flows into the Silver River (Photo by Bruce Mozert, Florida Archives).

again as flowing springs, refilling ancient channels carved during much earlier times. Consistent and ample rainfall and groundwater recharge started the most recent re-colonization by Florida's native springs' flora and fauna.

For the past 10,000 years or so, springs have been flowing in response to high and low aquifer levels resulting from wet periods and droughts. Before the 20th century, essentially all recharge to the FAS exited via springs and seeps. The freshwater portion of the FAS rests like a water-filled bubble on the underlying saltwater-filled aquifer and is bounded by saltwater along the east and west coastlines of peninsular Florida. When recharge was high, spring flow was high and *vice versa*. Limited written descriptions of spring flow before the early 20th Century, combined with the earliest spring flow data recorded by the U.S. Geological Survey in the early 1900s, lead us to conclude that 100 years ago many of the largest springs had consistently high flows, during wet and dry years due to a super abundance of recharge to and storage in the FAS.

By the 1940s there was growing evidence that spring flows were declining faster than could be explained by periodic droughts. By the 1980s it became evident at even the largest of springs in Florida (e.g., Silver, Rainbow, and Springs Creek) that average spring flows were lower than previously measured. The obvious culprit was the exponential increase in groundwater withdrawals following the introduction of drilled wells and diesel and electric pumps by the early 20th century.

By 1985, Silver Springs, once the mightiest spring in Florida and the U.S., and possibly in the world, was losing flow faster than neighboring Rainbow Springs. By 1998 Silver's annual average flow had dropped below Rainbow's annual average flow and has remained lower every year since. Both of these formerly beautiful springs are now suffering from greatly reduced average flows and more than 20- to 40-fold increases in nitrate nitrogen, principally as a result of agricultural and urban fertilizer uses. Both are undergoing a type of springs' eutrophication, the process that aquatic ecosystems go through in response to reduced flows and increased nutrients. Both of these springs are losing their native tapegrass and eelgrass and both are being overrun by filamentous algae. Their entire biology is changing as their primary producers, the base of the food pyramid, shift from an adapted and diverse assemblage of submerged aquatic vegetation, to a near monoculture of weedy algae species.

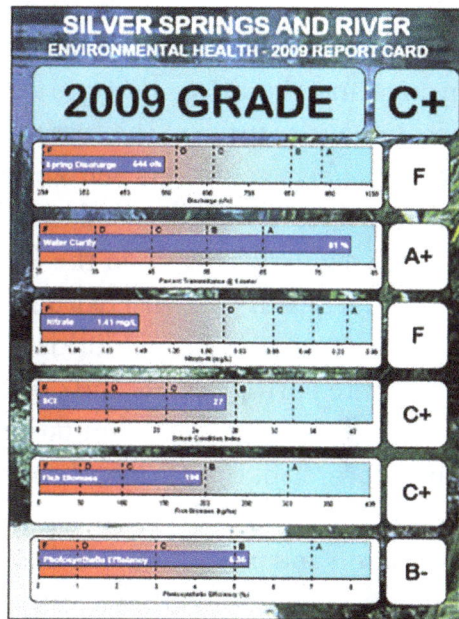

In spite of this man-made springs tragedy, in 2011 the State of Florida stopped funding springs science, education, and restoration. The private, non-profit Florida Springs Institute was founded to fulfill a dream of

Howard T. Odum and to help fill this gap in support for springs science and restoration.

With the financial meltdown and loss of State funding, much of the springs monitoring in Florida was discontinued. The Springs Institute is continuing critical monitoring as funds and man-power allow. Over the past 10 years the Springs Institute has continued collection of ecosystem-level data from Silver Springs and the Silver River to document the changing health for this most famous of springs. The Institute also initiated a SPRINGS WATCH program where volunteers help collect routine data at Silver and Ichetucknee Springs not otherwise collected by State agencies. Water quality trend data are regularly posted on the Institute's website to allow the public to follow the health of their favorite springs.

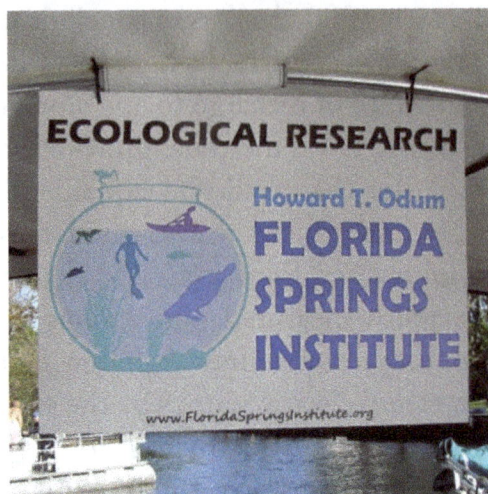

The Howard T. Odum Florida Springs Institute is currently operating with limited private funds and donated time. While the absence of public funding places significant limitations on how much the Springs Institute can accomplish, it has the advantage of allowing the Institute to take positions that are politically unpopular but absolutely critical for springs restoration and protection. The best science is essential to make informed management decisions. The Florida Springs Institute strives to use the most reliable information in order to develop sound recommendations to share with public officials with regulatory power. The Institute cooperates with university and state/federal agency scientists to refine technical understanding of the Floridan Aquifer and its spring discharges.

The future of the Florida Springs Institute is as uncertain as the future of Florida's springs. There is no doubt that the State of Florida needs a prestigious center for springs research, education, and development of effective springs management and restoration guidelines. The combined direct and indirect value of Florida's springs on the State's economy is likely more than one billion dollars per year. More important than their dollar value is the fact that springs provide a direct view into the Floridan

Aquifer System, which provides over 90% of the State's supply of freshwater and is arguably the most important natural resource in Florida. Clean and abundant groundwater is the lifeblood for Florida's economy and natural environment. Due to weak enforcement of existing Florida law, our groundwater is no longer abundant or clean. The view into the aquifer is cloudy. The Florida Springs Institute is attempting to shine a bright light into that murky darkness so the public and their representatives will make the right decisions to restore our groundwater and springs.

Florida Springs Institute staff and volunteers conducting a Silver Springs fish count in February 2020 (photo by author).

JACK MCEARCHERN DID IT ALL AT SILVER SPRINGS

Story by Marian Rizzo/ Correspondent
(Reprinted from the June 21, 2013, article in the Ocala Star-Banner Newspaper)

John "Jack" McEarchern Jr. has lost track of how many times he was killed, maimed or speared during filming of Lloyd Bridges' *Sea Hunt* TV series at Silver Springs. "I was a good guy, bad guy, dead guy, whatever they needed," McEarchern said.

"One time, I played the bad guy and rolled a rock on him (Bridges). Then, I turned around and played the good guy and saved him. "In another episode, they needed a dead guy on the bottom," he said. "They zoomed

Jack McEarchern Jr., talks about the days he used to dive at the Silver Springs Attraction in Silver Springs, Fla., on Thursday, June 13, 2013. McEarchern worked in public relations at the attraction for 10 years and was also a diver featured in over 100 "Sea Hunt" television episodes. Many of the underwater scenes for the show were shot at the springs in the late '50s and early '60s.
(Jacqui Janetzko/Star-Banner Correspondent)

in on me to start the show. It got so cold, I couldn't stop shaking, so they had to rewrite the script to say, 'He was in his death throes.' The best thing was getting out after eight hours under water. Seventy-two degrees will suck the heat right out of you."

The 155 episodes, which aired from 1958 to 1961, starred Bridges as salvage diver Mike Nelson. McEarchern chuckled when recalling Bridges' first underwater photo shoot. "He was scared to death," he said. "When that flashbulb went off, he came out of that water like somebody'd shot at him. But he became one of the most knowledgeable salvage divers in the country. He had to. He'd meet with these crowds, and he knew somebody was going to ask him questions. He said, 'I have to have the answers.'"

~

Like so many of the people who contributed to the colorful history of Silver Springs, McEarchern was born and bred here and spent much of his youth immersed in the springs' chilly waters.

The oldest of three boys, he attended elementary schools in Fairfield, Reddick and Ocala, and graduated from Ocala High School in 1949. He learned to swim underwater long before he donned scuba gear, and he worked as a lifeguard at Silver Springs when the park had a public beach.

McEarchern's photo album features shots of movie stars who came to Silver Springs, photos of himself diving, fishing and posing for ads, and two honorary certificates—one for the "Royal & Mysterious Order of the Silver Springs AquaSnobs" and the other a 1957 "Certificate of Unique Achievement" that also lists the names of former employee Ricou Browning and pioneering underwater photographer Bruce Mozert.

While leafing through the album, McEarchern paused at a photo of his wife, Joyce, and he teared up. Married on Sept. 24, 1949, they were together for more than 50 years.

"We were two 19-year-olds, madly in love," he said. "I let her be 19 for one month, then I married her. I didn't want folks to say I was robbing the cradle."

The McEarcherns had two sons, John III and Ben, and a daughter, Rita Carolyn.

Joyce died following a stroke 11 years ago.

His son John III was 14 when he participated in the making of a *Mike and the Mermaid* TV special, making him the youngest scuba diving stunt person ever at Silver Springs, McEarchern said.

For John III, his relationship with his father had many high points, whether under the sea or on land.

"He made sure us two boys had a good upbringing out in nature and in the woods," he said. "We hunted and fished a lot. He said to always work hard and be aware of nature. My dad's a hoot. I've had a million heart attacks in my life, and they was all from him. He'd sneak up behind ya and, 'Gotcha!' It was a good childhood. We had fun."

Aside from his work at Silver Springs park, McEarchern served as the fire chief of Silver Springs and worked in maintenance at Six Gun Territory and Rainbow Springs.

~

McEarchern learned scuba diving from the late Newt Perry, best known as a stand-in for Johnny Weissmuller in the *Tarzan* films and for developing the Weeki Wachee Springs attraction.

McEarchern was first called to Silver Springs by his friend, the late Bill Ray, who was head of public relations at the time. Then an installer with the Florida Telephone Co., McEarchern was asked to hook up an underwater phone for a project of WMOP radio.

"Vern Arnette was the announcer," McEarchern said. "He called UPS and told them he was under water. They called him a liar."

McEarchern later worked in public relations at Silver Springs for 10 years. His jobs ranged from scuba diving to fixing broken things to serving sodas in the commissary. He also posed for magazine ads and billboards, helped catch alligators, "noodled" bass with his bare hands, leaped off a barge to explore underwater springs and rubbed elbows with the stars— Arlene Francis, Hugh Downs and Gregory Peck, among them.

Movie-making wasn't always glamorous, but it was always interesting. He recalled a time when a movie crew needed a fox for a scene, McEarchern said they found a dead one on the road and then posed him the way they wanted. When he wasn't helping pose road-kill, McEarchern was wrangling larger, livelier predators during alligator roundups with Browning and the public relations team.

"We captured an alligator in the forest and needed to move him,"

McEarchern recalled. "We tied him up, rolled him up in a tarp, loaded him up in Bruce Mozert's station wagon and toted him home."

When the University of Florida needed an Albert the Alligator mascot for a Gators football rally, McEarchern helped transport the beast to Gainesville.

"I got a rope around his neck," he said. "Don Shaw came up on his back and slammed his mouth shut, then I went up there and put a rope around it. We put plywood in the back of a pickup truck and threw the gator in there. When we got to the university's park, we cut the rope and his mouth went open. We walked him around the park and people scattered. In 30 seconds we had that gator all to ourselves."

In a phone interview from his home near Fort Lauderdale, Browning talked about the team's relocation of nuisance alligators.

"We were hired to capture alligators in the lakes in St. Petersburg," Browning said. "We got a whole bunch of us together to go down and take them away from peoples' homes. They probably took 'em back to the Springs. Ross Allen was there at the time."

Browning said he knew McEarchern both on the job and socially.

"The main thing I remember was Jack was a kind of jack-of-all-trades," Browning said. "He could do almost anything mechanically. Everything we did, he would be involved in any of the physical activities of the project, whatever it might be. He was extremely helpful in every project we did at Silver Springs, publicity wise, and he helped build things and fix things."

David Faison, who has been a glass-bottom boat driver for 55 years, recalled McEarchern's penchant for fishing.

"He was the baddest man," Faison said with a grin. "He caught all the fish. No wonder we got no fish in there. He was an outside guy, liked to fish and hunt. That was his cup of tea."

∽

McEarchern has seen transformational changes at Silver Springs. He was there when the only ride was the famed glass-bottom boats and the only sidewalk followed the river along its north side.

In the early 1960s, the park's owners sold it to the American Broadcasting Company, ushering in the corporate era at Silver Springs that continues to this day.

Each corporate owner expanded the offerings at the park, grafting rides and other attractions onto its natural-Florida theme.

ABC added Wild Waters water park in 1978; Florida Leisure Acquisition Corp. opened Jeep Safari and Lost River Voyage and added the Garlits car museum; and Ogden Entertainment debuted World of Bears, Kids Ahoy! Playland and the Twister flume, along with a host of news shows and exhibits.

But many of McEarchern's fondest memories involve the springs themselves. He recalls the rhesus monkeys that S. Colonel Tooey, owner of the Jungle cruise, helped bring to the park. The boat captains, he said, would toss bananas and bread to them until, in recent years, the monkeys became too aggressive and had to be moved.

"One boat captain was trying to get a monkey to take a banana. That big ol' bull jumped on him and tore up his chest," he said. "Another time, a female came on there, and them boys just gave her that boat."

Jack McEarchern Jr., right, is seen in a scrapbook alligator wrangling as he talks about the days he used to dive at the Silver Springs Attraction in Silver Springs, Fla., on Thursday, June 13, 2013. McEarchern worked in public relations at the attraction for 10 years and was also a diver featured in over 100 "Sea Hunt" television episodes. Many of the underwater scenes for the show were shot at the springs in the late '50s and early '60s. (Jacqui Janetzko/Star-Banner Correspondent)

He also recalled with mixed emotions the separate beaches at the park that marked the segregation-era.

While he never agreed with segregation, he says the beaches were a major draw for locals and provided years of good memories for visitors. There was one beach for the whites and one for the blacks "at Paradise Park, down where the glass bottom boats turn around," he said. "They had their own beauty shows and parties and everything down there."

When ABC took over, they closed down the beaches and made other changes, McEarchern said.

"Everything was running fine till then," he said. "They took over and fired everybody. They let Bill Ray go. As far as I'm concerned, that was a big mistake. He was responsible for getting 'Sea Hunt' and getting all our diving equipment, wet suits, swimming gear, everything. He got Mercury Motors' advertising. Bill Ray was PR. He didn't wait for them to come to us. He went to them and talked them into coming to Silver Springs.

"If somebody asked me to rename Silver Springs, I'd call it Bill Blue Ray's Florida Silver Springs," McEarchern said. "He made it. The rest of us just worked there."

SILVER SPRINGS AND THE FOUNTAIN OF YOUTH

Robert L. Knight, Ph.D., Howard T. Odum Florida Springs Institute
(This piece first appeared in *Aquiferious* by Margaret Ross Tolbert)

Try to remember the first Florida spring you ever visited—Silver, Wakulla, Ichetucknee, Wekiwa, Blue, Rainbow, Crystal, etc. If you saw your first spring more than 25 to 30 years ago, you probably witnessed an illuminated, crystal clear bowl; ethereal blue home to long green waving grasses, suspended fish, turtles, and manatees; open portal to the dark underworld and source of the never-ending water of life; water so frigid in summer it gave chill-bumps, flow so strong that it boiled to the surface, Nature so pure that you thought you were in Florida's Eden.

One-hundred-and-fifty years ago an intrepid professor from the University of South Carolina decided to visit Silver Springs because of the "extraordinary reports" he had heard in relation to its optical properties. Professor John Le Conte (1818-1891) visited Silver Springs in December 1859 and provided the first known detailed account of this "remarkable Silver-Spring." In Professor Le Conte's own words:

"The most remarkable and interesting phenomenon presented by this Spring, is the truly extraordinary transparency of the water; in this respect surpassing anything which can be imagined. On a clear and calm day, after the sun has

First glass-bottom boat at Silver Springs (Florida Archives).

14

attained sufficient altitude, the view from the side of a small boat floating on the surface of the water near the center of the head-spring, is beautiful beyond description, and well calculated to produce a powerful impression upon the imagination. Every feature and configuration of the bottom of this gigantic basin is as distinctly visible as if the water was removed, and the atmosphere substituted in its place!

"A larger portion of the bottom of this pool is covered with a luxuriant growth of species of water-grass, and gigantic moss-like plants, which attain a height of three to four feet. Without doubt, the development of so vigorous a vegetation at such depths, is owing to the large amount of solar light which penetrates these waters. The sunlight illuminated the sides and bottom of this remarkable pool as brilliantly as if nothing obstructed the light. The shadows of our little boat, of our overhanging heads and hats, of projecting crags and logs, of the surrounding forest, and of the vegetation at the bottom, were distinctly and sharply defined; while the constant waving of the slender and delicate moss-like

Arrilla Jones highlighting the incredible underwater clarity looking through a telescope at Silver Springs (1962 by Bruce Mozert, Florida Archives).

15

plants, by means of the currents created by the boiling up of the water, and the swimming of numerous fish above this miniature subaqueous forest, imparted a living reality to the scene which never can be forgotten. On a bright day, the beholder seems to be looking down from some lofty airy point on a truly fairy scene in the immense basin beneath him: a scene whose beauty and magical effect are vastly enhanced by the chromatic tints with which it is invested!"

Professor Le Conte's description goes on in a surprisingly detailed and accurate account of why the clarity and very existence of Silver Springs is dependent upon its geography, located in a natural basin where all drainage is "subterranean" and that:

"… it is obvious that all the water which falls on this hydrographic basin boils up in the Silver-Spring after having been strained, filtered, and decolorized in its passage through beds of sand and tortuous underground channels."

Professor Le Conte continues with:

"Doubtless there are many other springs to be found in the State of Florida, whose waters possess the same optical properties as those of the Silver-Spring; although perhaps, their transparency may be less perfect. The 'Suwanee Spring' is said to exhibit analogous phenomena; and the famous fountain situated ten miles from Tallahassee, called Wachulla or Wakulla, is represented as 'an immense limestone basin, as yet unfathomed in the center, with waters as transparent as crystal.'"

Former extraordinary fish abundance and diversity in Silver Springs (c1955 photo by Bruce Mozert, Florida Archives).

Professor Le Conte saw something 150 years ago that no modern living person has seen, namely a Florida spring totally unaffected by electric groundwater pumps, water bottling plants, sewage treatment plants, stormwater pipes, septic tanks, and packaged fertilizers. With about 18 million people currently living in Florida, it is rare to see a spring that is not disturbed by human activities. The majority of our springs are impaired by increases in nutrients and reductions in flow and water clarity. Their plants are trampled from recreation, they are home to exotic invasive species, and their water is green and less transparent.

Luckily for me, I saw the "Silver-Springs" through the glass bottom boats 56 years ago. Like John Le Conte I was able to experience the sight of numerous fish apparently suspended in mid-air. I personally remember the former clarity of those blue-tinged waters, the purity of the lush waving grasses, and the pageant of fish and turtles in their watery Eden. While Silver Springs was certainly altered in some ways in 1954 when I first visited, it was easy at that time to agree to the letter with the description provided a century earlier by Professor Le Conte.

Also in 1954, another young professor, Dr. Howard T. Odum, newly hired by the University of Florida in Gainesville, was conducting a detailed ecological study at Silver Springs. Dr. Odum's study was comprehensive in a way new to science at the time—he and his scientific colleagues studied the whole Silver Springs ecosystem, quantifying the inflows and outflows of energy, describing the structure and function of the plant community, counting the numbers and estimating the weights of all of the aquatic animals, and even evaluating the effect of the humans on the ecosystem as they drove the glass bottom boats and fed bread to the fish throughout the year. Dr. Odum's epic study of the ecology of Silver Springs became one of the most widely recognized scientific monographs worldwide in the biological sciences and helped to establish a new paradigm in ecology that emphasizes the need to measure energy flows to be able to understand and predict the responses of ecosystems.

After a productive academic career developing the new scientific discipline of Systems Ecology and studying and comparing the energy flows in tropical rain forests, coral reefs, and shallow marine bays, Dr. Odum returned to Gainesville and the University of Florida in 1970. Over the next eight years while on class field trips to Silver Springs with his annual course in Systems Ecology, Dr. Odum noted that the formerly abundant fish in the spring boil and spring run had apparently declined in numbers since his original studies in the 1950s. When I came to the University of Florida to work on my doctorate degree in the late 1970s, Dr. Odum suggested that I re-study Silver Springs to try to learn more about the possible effects of the declining fish populations on the overall Silver Springs ecosystem.

During my two years of field work at Silver Springs, while I was literally immersed in the underwater world of aquatic ecology, I experienced the majesty and complexity of a spring ecosystem. Springs offer a nearly ideal

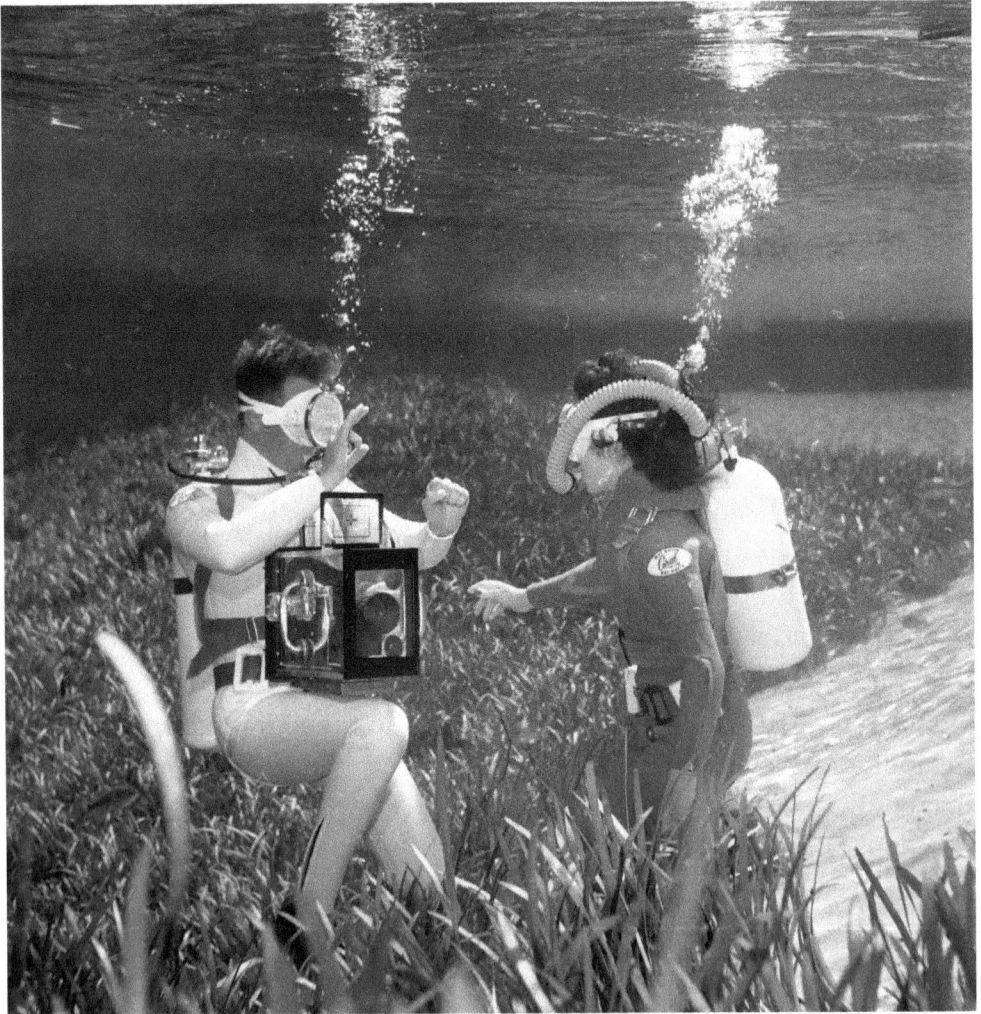

Scuba divers in dense native aquatic plant bed in Silver Springs about 1950 (Bruce Mozert photo, Florida Archives).

laboratory for research. Unlike most other aquatic environments that are highly variable with respect to flows and water quality, many artesian springs are nearly thermostatic (constant temperature), chemostatic (constant chemistry), hydrostatic (relatively constant water flow and depth), and as if that is not enough, the water is so clear year-round, that it is easy to see what most of the flora and fauna are doing during their daily and nocturnal routines, making it relatively easy to study their numbers and behavior. The only major external "forcing function" in clear artesian springs that is not constant is the input of sunlight, it cycles on and off daily and varies with the seasons over an annual period. In most aquatic environments it is next to impossible to develop a clear understanding of the interactions between ecosystem components and it is almost never possible to repeat experiments under identical environmental conditions. Not so in springs. As Dr. Odum stated in his landmark monograph on Silver Springs:

"Most terrible and healthy for the poor ecologist is the realization that anyone can check his field work at any later time, a rare situation indeed heretofore."

Dr. Odum selected Silver Springs for my research partly to test the validity of this claim he had made 25 years before.

In his original work, Dr. Odum was especially interested in the factors that control primary productivity or "power" in ecosystems. It was his supposition that top carnivores and other consumers near the top of the food chain in natural ecosystems provide essential feedback actions that help to maximize ecosystem productivity. The theory was that consumer populations are adjusted to levels that consume just the right amount of food so that the population of each lower group of consumers in the food chain is in turn controlled to just the right level to control the one below, right down to the community of primary producers (plants and algae). If the animals that graze on plants (herbivores) are too numerous and eat too many plants, then their population suffers from overexploitation of their food source. If there are too few herbivores, then the plants are not cropped often enough to keep them in their optimal actively growing stage and the plants senesce and produce less food for the herbivores. It takes just the right population of grazers to maximize the productivity of the plants. But the herbivores will have widely fluctuating populations and create a boom-bust economy if their populations are only controlled by their food resources. For this reason, it takes just the right population of primary carnivores (animals that feed on herbivores) to maintain the optimal population of herbivores. And it takes just the right number of top carnivores to maintain the optimal number of mid-level consumers.

Dr. Odum's ecological systems theory indicates that this fine tuning takes place at

Silver Springs native aquatic eelgrass covered by overgrowth of noxious filamentous algae and being replaced by hydrilla, an invasive, non-native aquatic plant species (Photo 2020 by the author).

every level of the food chain and throughout entire ecosystems and other stable and mature systems of all types. When an ecosystem achieves this finely balanced chain of feedback loops, primary production at the base of the food chain is at its maximum sustainable level and the overall "power" of the ecosystem is maximized. My task was to develop an experimental project that could test this theory at Silver Springs.

Dr. Odum had previously quantified the extremely high primary productivity of Silver Springs and the spring ecosystem's almost perfect balance between primary producers (plants) and consumers (animals and microbes). The Silver Springs ecosystem studied by Professors Le Conte and Odum had been "self-designing" under relatively constant environmental forcing functions for thousands of years and had likely reached its potential for maximizing productivity. However, at an accelerating rate, human activities such as the construction of the Rodman Dam downstream from Silver Springs on the Ocklawaha River, were changing these forcing functions, blocking the movement of migrating fish and manatees via the St. Johns River from the Atlantic Ocean to Silver Springs and possibly resulting in the observed reduction of the fish populations in the spring. The striped mullet and channel catfish so numerous in the 1950s disappeared shortly after the Rodman Dam was closed in 1968. The loss of these formerly high fish populations appeared to offer an experiment to test the hypothesized negative effect of a lower population of consumers on spring ecosystem productivity. Theory predicted that the productivity of the whole spring run plant community might be reduced in the late 1970s compared to the rates of plant growth measured by Dr. Odum in the 1950s. My pleasant job as a graduate student was to repeat the same types of measurements of whole ecosystem productivity that Dr. Odum had made 25 years before.

It turns out that measuring the productivity and respiration of all of the plants and animals in a flowing spring and spring run is easier than it sounds. All one must do is continuously measure the amount of dissolved oxygen upstream and downstream and then calculate the change in mass of that essential element over time. The oxygen that is dissolved in the water is produced by the aquatic plants through the process of photosynthesis during the day and is consumed to meet the metabolic requirements of the plants and animals day and night. Just like any plant or animal these changes are a measure of the "breathing" or "metabolism" of a spring "super organism." On a daily basis the predictable rise and fall of oxygen dissolved in the spring water looks just like a human's heartbeat on a cardiogram.

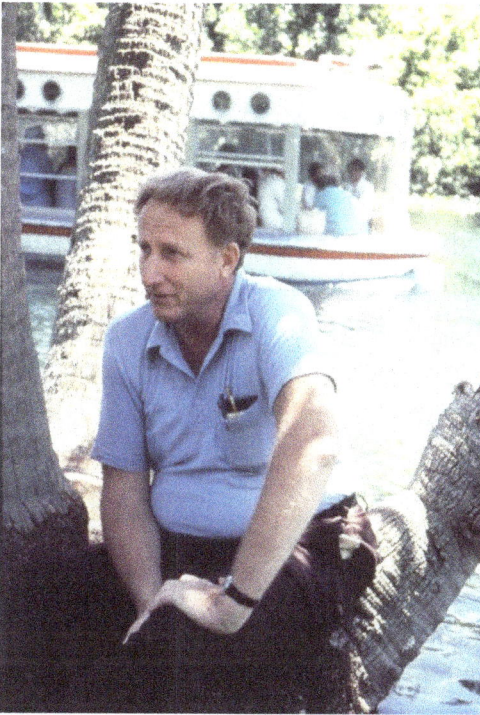

Dr. Howard T. Odum supervising the author's re-study of Silver Springs in 1979 (photo by the author).

Although I had previously seen this phenomenon described in textbooks, it was a transcendental experience when I measured it for myself. During the daylight hours, I could watch the concentration of dissolved oxygen in the spring water change using a field meter. As the sun rose in the sky on a clear day, the amount of oxygen in the water rose in perfect synchrony. When the day waned after high noon the rate of increase declined. When a cloud passed over the sun for a few minutes the rate of oxygen change would slow or stop, or actually start to decline. When the sun set, the rate of oxygen change was negative and remained negative until the sun rose again the next morning. Just like a doctor with a stethoscope I was literally watching the breathing of a living organism! The spring was clearly much more than its living parts, it had at least one of the same emergent properties of a highly organized organism, it was converting calories from the sun into production of an organized system of inter-dependent plants and animals that displayed remarkable stability over time.

My measurements demonstrated that Silver Springs was operating very much like it had the last time it was tested, 25 years before! The overall primary productivity of the upper three quarters mile of the Silver River in 1979-80 was very similar to Dr. Odum's earlier estimates. This productivity was very high, comparable to tropical rain forests, coral reef ecosystems, and highly managed cornfields. Primary productivity in Silver springs was still high during my study, in spite of an apparent decline in fish mass of about 78 percent. However, my fish counts indicated that there had been a compensating increase in the population density of gizzard shad, a fish species that feeds primarily on algae. Did these measurements disprove Dr. Odum's maximum power theory and the idea of consumer control, or did they perhaps indicate that the Silver Springs ecology was resilient and had adapted to the changes in fish populations over the ten-year period since the dam was constructed?

Further tests were warranted to see if short-term consumer population adjustments could affect control of productivity at Silver Springs. I needed to set up experimental units that could mimic the larger Silver River ecosystem to artificially manipulate populations of consumer organisms and measure the resulting levels of primary productivity. I was able to accomplish this by the use of "mesocosms" or small constructed spring ecosystems that could be deployed in the river, naturally colonize with a flora and fauna similar to the larger spring ecosystem and be replicated and manipulated experimentally. Each mesocosm was a polyethylene tube 18 feet long and four inches in diameter. By deploying these mesocosms in the river, Silver Springs water flowed through them from one end to the other. I was able to control consumer densities in these mesocosms by use of screens over their open upstream and downstream ends. After these tubes colonized with periphytic diatoms (attached algae that naturally grow on the tapegrass in spring runs) and the small invertebrates that feed on that periphyton, I introduced either snails (herbivores) or small mosquitofish (carnivores) at differing known densities to each mesocosm (including controls with no snails or fish), and measured their upstream-downstream changes in dissolved oxygen for two to three weeks. In this way I could directly assess the effect of differing consumer densities on productivity of the periphytic algae in the spring run mesocosms.

Voila! Productivity (ecosystem power) was maximized in the experimental mesocosms at intermediate consumer densities comparable to the densities that occur in the real spring run. Dr. Odum wasn't surprised but I was impressed. It was a eureka moment for me when I saw for myself that Nature could be so well behaved and follow her own laws. Dr. Odum had figured this out for himself years before. But just like so many other young people, I had to see it for myself before I could truly believe it. Silver Springs was like a finely tuned automobile purring with great power. Her reduced fish populations had required her to re-organize and adapt to the

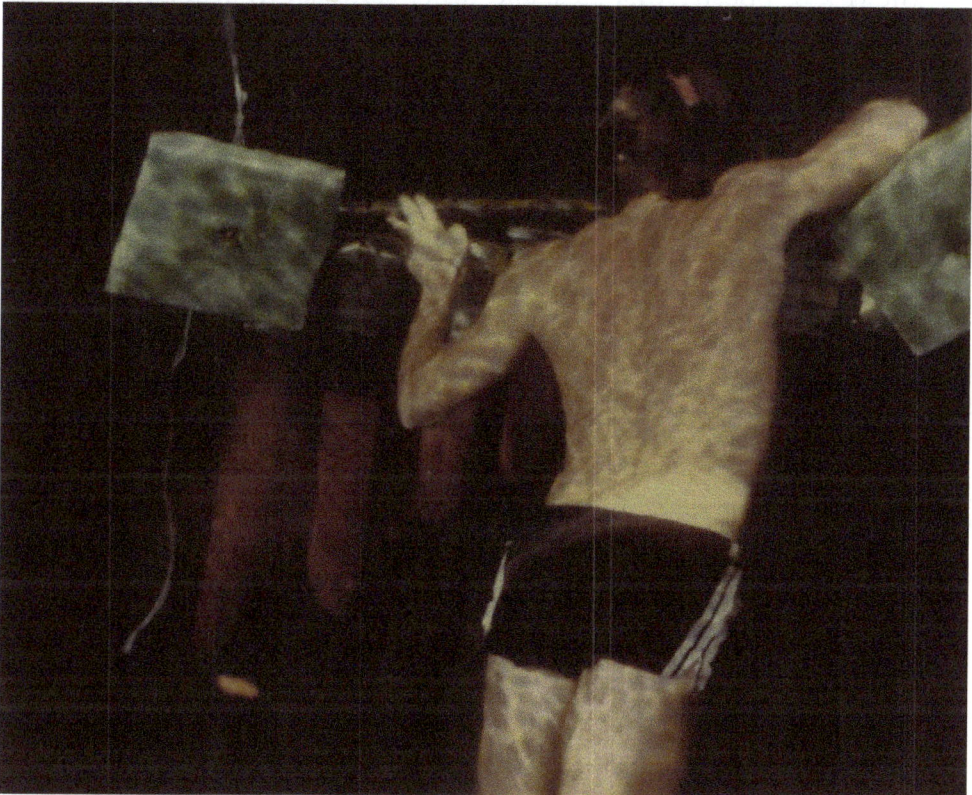

The author conducting his Silver Springs mesocosm study of the effects of consumer organisms (snails and fish) on optimal primary productivity in 1979 (Photo by Gail Knight).

new external forces acting on her (the Rodman Dam), and she had maintained her power output and was still majestic in her overall performance. The heartbeat of Silver Springs, this giant "super organism," whose living lifeblood (water) in her upper three-fourths of a mile weighs more than 136,000 tons, whose living plants and animals in this study reach weigh more than 1,400 tons, and whose gross plant productivity (power output) is equivalent to about 9,000 tons of living tissue per year, had survived and adapted to the first major human alteration in her broader support system.

Tragically, even at the time I was conducting my doctoral research at Silver Springs 30 years ago, there were the first signs of cancer in her veins. The concentration of nitrate nitrogen issuing from the Floridan Aquifer and feeding the ecology of Silver Springs had nearly doubled between Dr. Odum's study and my own. There is no doubt that the increase in this plant-growth nutrient was fueling a different kind of change at Silver Springs. As excess sugar intake changes a child's metabolism and heightens the risk of obesity, diabetes, and other serious physical ailments, the increase in nitrate in the source water to Silver Springs may have resulted in shifts in plant communities in the spring run as early as the 1970s, and is plainly evident today. The populations of algae were shifting from the beneficial periphytic diatoms that formerly provided the food for the rest of the aquatic food chain, to filamentous green and blue-green algae with little palatability to herbivorous animals. These filamentous algae are the weeds of polluted water systems. A 50-year retrospective study conducted at Silver Springs in 2005 found that the populations of these weedy algae have increased from below detection in the 1950s, to more than half of the overall plant biomass 50 years later. During this time, the concentration of nitrate nitrogen had increased by 160 percent. Continuing with the sugar analogy above, this nitrate was making the plant community heavier but not stronger or more powerful. During the 50-year retrospective study in 2004 and 2005, there were fewer fish at Silver Springs and the ecosystem metabolism was lower than it had been 25 and 50 years before.

Based on my own observations of the changes occurring at Silver Springs and at other springs around north Florida, I have no doubt that we have lost or are losing one of the most important and unique natural resources in our state. Our Fountains of Youth symbolize the purity of our drinking water and our natural world. I am sure that many people can live without springs in Florida, but the question we should all ask is: do we want to? Springs will recover if we make decisive changes in how we are living on this land. The cost of these necessary changes is not great, in fact those necessary changes are likely to save money in some cases as we conserve fertilizers and the power costs of pumping too much water from the aquifer. It is my opinion that the time is ripe to make the changes we need to reclaim our state's natural heritage, to bring back the remarkable clarity and power of our spring ecosystems, and to return the Fountain of Youth to Florida's Eden.

THREE MEN
150 YEARS OF PILOTING GLASS-BOTTOM BOATS AT SILVER SPRINGS

Story by Marian Rizzo/ Correspondent
(Reprinted from the June 27, 2013 article in the Ocala Star-Banner Newspaper)

Davewis Faison is one of three boat captains who together have logged more than 150 years of service at the Silver Springs Attraction.
Faison stepped around the outside ledge of his glass-bottom boat and slipped into the driver's seat with the agility of a much younger man. At

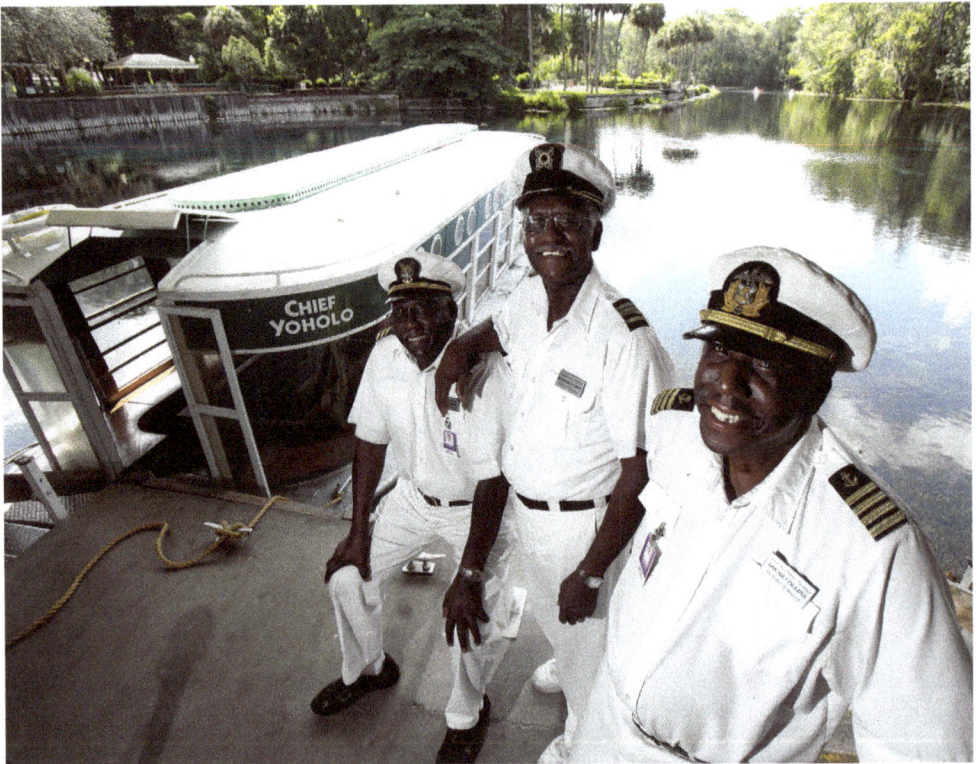

Silver Springs Boat Captains David Faison, left, Roosevelt Faison, center, and Oscar Collins, right, have over 150 years experience between the three of them as Boat Captains on the World Famous Glass Bottom Boats at Silver Springs Attraction Wednesday morning, June 19, 2013. (Doug Engle/Ocala Star-Banner)2013

81, Faison has put in 55 years as a boat captain, and his spiel reveals his knowledge of the Silver River and the wildlife that lives there.

Faison is one of three boat captains who together have logged more than 150 years of service at the Silver Springs attraction. His brother, Roosevelt, 76, has worked there for 57 years, and their brother-in-law, Oscar Collins, 67, has put in 44 years and is the lead captain.

David Faison said he doesn't know what he will do with his time if he can't stay on after the park is integrated into the state park system in October.

"I'm a pretty healthy man," David Faison said. "I don't know what they're going to do, or what they're planning, but these boats for sure are gonna be runnin'. Who's gonna run 'em, I don't know."

Visitors to Silver Springs can opt to board the glass-bottom boats for a 25-minute cruise of the river. While gliding over the crystal-clear surface, people who have never scuba dived are able to enter an underwater world of fish, turtles, spiked river grass and deep crevices that spew out thousands of gallons of water every day.

All the while, the boat captains give a brief history of the river and point out such items as a dugout canoe that has sat on the river floor for decades, statues that served as movie props in the making of the "I Spy" television series and the James Bond film *Moonraker* and, along the river's edge, alligators lolling in the sun next to a row of turtles sunbathing on a fallen log.

The Good Ol' Days

For the three veteran boat captains, fond memories abound.

"The spring's water is just as clear and just as beautiful as it was 57 years ago," Roosevelt Faison said. "One of the highlights was back in the days when we had what we called a 'fish football game.' We'd drop this big wad of bread down there. The bream we named the 'Army,' and the catfish were the 'Navy.' The Army would just move the dough ball around, but the Navy could put it in their mouth. That's why they always won.

"Though fewer in number these days, the river's fish population still includes gar, bluegill, bream, catfish and bass, but not as many.

"That's one of my disappointments, the fish leaving and a lot more algae growing," Roosevelt Faison said. "Years ago, you could stand on the dock and look out on the river and the eel grass would glow, that's how shiny it was. Now, it's covered with algae. When the state comes in, I'd like to see them come out with a barge and a net and start cleaning up the algae. It'll take years to clean it up. I won't see it in my lifetime."

The Faisons and Collins grew up together in Fort McCoy, and Collins married the Faisons' sister. Roosevelt was the first of the three to take a job at Silver Springs. David followed within a couple years and, 10 years later, the brothers helped train Collins.

The captains receive Coast Guard training, with some limitations, Collins said. "The toughest thing was docking," he said. "These boats have a flat bottom, so they operate different from any other boat, especially on windy days. I had some bump the dock. My brother-in-law trained me to dock the boat and do a good job with it. I can do it with my eyes closed now."

David Faison laughs about the first time he tried to walk around the outside ledge on his boat to get inside, the only way a captain can get past a crowd of visitors.

"I didn't have but two inches to walk on, and, oo-ee, I hit the water," he said. "I just lost my balance and I turned around and jumped for the dock. I come up out of the water, stepped back on the boat and carried 'em off down the river."

Occasionally, the unexpected happens, such as Collins' recollection of the day his boat passed over an alligator lying on the river bottom.

"That's unusual," he said. "Most of the time, they're on the bank. The people couldn't believe it. Some people think they're not real until they make a move."

Local folks might remember the Silver Springs billboards that once stood along the highway. Collins said he was the one waving from the boat in the blown-up photo. The same image also was on the front of the park's promotional T-shirts at the time, he said.

Five decades of transitions

During their careers at Silver Springs, the Faisons and Collins saw the park change hands numerous times, starting with the joint ownership of Carl Ray and W.M. Davidson. According to the Silver Springs website, the property was owned by the American Broadcasting Company and Florida Leisure Attractions, which sold it to the state in 1993 but continued to manage the attraction through a lease agreement. The lease passed to Ogden Entertainment in 1996 and to Palace Entertainment in 2002.

"The best days were in the '70s," Roosevelt Faison said. "That's when we had more attendance here. There was Six Gun Territory and Rainbow Springs down in Dunnellon. It was something to get off the interstate for them three parks. Then we lost Six Gun, and the state took over Rainbow Springs. And Disney drew people to Orlando."

The Silver Springs website also describes the evolution of the glass-bottom boat, which was designed by Hullam Jones in 1878. Also in the late 1870s, Phillip Morell, a resident of Silver Springs, built a glass-bottom rowboat and sold rides above the springs.

Silver Springs acquired its glass-bottom boats around the turn of the 20th century. In 1909, C. "Ed" Carmichael installed cushioned seats and canopies. The early gasoline engines were converted to electric in 1932.

Collins said the former boats were made of wood and had Carl Ray's family names painted on them. The newer versions are constructed of aluminum and bear Seminole Indian names.

"They were smaller back in the day," Collins said. "They carried about 25 people. Now they can carry 35."

Three of the boats are operating and 15 are on reserve. Each of the captains is paired with his own boat. Collins generally pilots the Chief Yoholo. David Faison drives the Chief Micanopy and Roosevelt drives the Chief Neameth.

"I'd like to see another boat ride come in here. The old standards were the glass-bottom boats and the Jungle Cruise," Collins said.

New challenge on the river

On a recent day, the three boat captains stood on the dock and watched with concern as several kayaks crisscrossed the river and paused over the head spring.

While Roosevelt Faison says kayaking can be fun, he fears the congestion could pose a challenge for the glass-bottom boats.

"We can see a difference already," he said. "The sale of kayaks went up, and everybody went out and bought one. They have the right-of-way because they don't have a motor. That puts the burden on us. They can see us, but we can't see them. They're supposed to stay out of our way, but we have to go around them not to hit them. They go down the springs and jump out of their boat and cloudy up the springs. They're not supposed to be swimming out there where we're running the boats."

"And, there's no fishing allowed," he added.

The Florida Department of Environmental Protection last month opened discussions with potential vendors to provide services at the park. DEP spokeswoman Dee Ann Miller said last week that talks with Ocala-based concessionaires to handle music concerts, special events and a recreational service are ongoing. Those firms include Diversified Event Productions, a concert promoter that seeks to use the Twin Oaks Mansion at Silver Springs for up to 22 concerts a year; What's Up Media, a special events coordinator; and Eco-Recreation Management, which operates Discovery Kayak Tours. She said the state also is working with possible concessionaires to provide food service and run the glass-bottom boats.

SILVER SPRINGS—DYING OF THIRST

Robert L. Knight, Ph.D., Howard T. Odum Florida Springs Institute
(Reprinted from the Gainesville Sun, May 2011)

Clear, pure groundwater is the basis for life in Florida's artesian springs. Remove flowing water and a spring is a sinkhole, a stagnant window into the dark limestone underworld. A spring's functionality or "life" declines when its flow decreases and increases in proportion to flow. The living assemblage of plants and animals characteristic of a Florida spring is directly dependent upon the quantity of groundwater that "springs" forth from its limestone vent.

Bird's eye view of Silver Springs in 1946 when flows were measured over 500 million gallons per day (Florida Archives).

Healthy springs are alive. They efficiently capture and convert Florida's abundant sunlight into plant and animal life. The waving eelgrass, sunfish, bass, turtles, alligators, manatees, otters, and birds that live in and around springs are the visible living parts of their watery environment. And just like all other living things, when springs are deprived of water, they become unhealthy and eventually die.

Before 1900, when Florida's human population was less than one million people, there were no electric-powered well pumps, and human consumption of groundwater was negligible compared to the natural recharge of rainfall to the aquifer. Also before 1900, Florida's springs had thousands of years of uninterrupted flow to nourish their complex and vast ecologies. The first Europeans who wrote about Florida's springs were astounded by these natural aquaria that were home to countless fish and wildlife.

Healthy springs attracted the human imagination and became Florida's first and most famous tourist attractions.

All life is dependent upon water, including human life. It takes from one to three days for an adult human to die from thirst. Symptoms of dehydration are extremely painful. An adult human needs to ingest about one gallon of freshwater per day to thrive.

Groundwater, the lifeblood of springs that once seemed infinite, is finite. When humans consume groundwater there is less flow at our springs. A gallon of groundwater consumed by humans is one less gallon for springs. A million gallons consumed by humans is a million fewer gallons for our springs and their dependent flora and fauna. The question for humans who wish to protect springs is: how much is too much? How much flow can a spring lose and still be healthy?

Marion County's Silver Springs showed no apparent declining flows until the 1980s. Arguably, once the best-known tourist attraction in Florida and the largest clear-water spring in the United States, Silver Springs recently received a failing grade for flow (an F based on an average 29 percent flow reduction) on its Springs Health Report Card, published by the Florida Springs Institute. The 29 percent average flow reduction in the country's largest spring is equal to 145 million gallons per day.

During the same monitoring period, Silver Glen, a spring that is relatively immune to human groundwater consumption due to its protected springshed located in the Ocala National Forest, had no apparent change in average flow.

As a first approximation, it is safe to say that Silver Springs has 29 percent less capacity to support aquatic life than it did forty or more years ago. As it loses its groundwater inflow, Silver Springs is literally dying a slow death.

State water managers recently announced that "Marion County should experience no water-supply issues for the next two decades." This is a surprising conclusion considering that flows at Silver Springs have been declining dramatically for nearly 30 years. It is the water management district's responsibility to establish a minimum flow for Silver Springs that will protect it from "significant harm." Their recent meeting with county officials appears to send a message that without a formal minimum flow determination, there is no regulatory protection for Silver Springs.

Concerned parents view a failing grade on their child's report card as a wake-up call to take strong action. As stewards of the health of our economic and natural resources, public officials should not ignore this failing grade or the plight of Silver Springs.

Curious West Indian Manatee photographed from a kayak on the Silver River in 2019. Manatees will return by the hundreds to the Silver River when the Rodman Dam is eventually removed, and the Ocklawaha River is restored. (photo by author).

EX-SILVER SPRINGS WORKER ENJOYED A WILD ADVENTURE

Story by Marian Rizzo/ Correspondent
(Reprinted from the July 6, 2013, article in the Ocala Star-Banner Newspaper)

Leon Cheatom stood beside a barbed-wire fence at the Marion County Sheriff's work farm and hollered "Heeup!" Almost immediately, a dozen cows scrambled from a pasture through a gate and made a beeline toward Cheatom, their eyes on the slice of bread in his hand. A captain with the Sheriff's Office, Cheatom works part time at the facility, assisting inmates with the care of the animals and the crops.

But six years ago, Cheatom was working in a different environment with a different kind of critters. Instead of cows, hogs and chickens, he

Marion County Sheriff Capt. Leon Cheatom talks about his lifelong career at Silver Springs as he spends time with cattle at the Sheriff's Work Camp in Ocala, FL on Tuesday June 25, 2013. Cheatom started at the springs at 14 and did every job there until the latest owner laid him off several years ago. (Alan Youngblood/OCALA STAR-BANNER 2013)

was handling snakes, alligators and the exotic wildlife that resided at the Silver Springs attraction. Today, he drives an all-terrain vehicle around the work farm; back then, he was tooling along the Silver River at the helm of a passenger-laden boat.

For Cheatom, the interaction with the cows and other animals at the work farm evoked memories of tossing bread to fish, teaching hogs to swim by luring them into the river and handing a banana into the waiting fingers of a rhesus monkey. To him, those were the good ole days at Silver Springs.

But after Palace Entertainment picked up the management lease at Silver Springs, Cheatom and several other longtime employees were laid-off. The assistant operations manager at the time, Cheatom was 69 years old and had worked at the park for 55 years.

Now 74, Cheatom recalled with bitterness the day Palace Entertainment General Manager Terry Turner announced their termination.

"He said we were laid-off. I said we were fired," Cheatom said. "He couldn't give a reason why they let us go."

In a 2007 Star-Banner article, Turner defended the decision.

"We have to be more efficient and, unfortunately, people get affected by cost savings," he said. "We went through the whole organization, and Leon's position was one that was eliminated."

Cheatom's career at Silver Springs began when he was 14 years old. He started working there after school and during weekends and vacations. His father was chief of security at the park, and his uncle and cousins also worked there. A product of Central Florida's natural environment, Cheatom was born Dec. 10, 1938, in a two-bedroom shack on the banks of the Ocklawaha River, just seven miles from the wildlife preserve.

"I was born where the big bridge on highway 40 is now," he said. "Back then, it was a small bridge, the kind that swung around. My mom was the bridge tender." Cheatom grew up with raccoons and an alligator named Charlie as companions.

"In school, my nickname was 'River Rat,'" he said, a tone of pride in his voice.

Cheatom was hired at Silver Springs by Colonel Tooey, a concessionaire who ran the Jungle Cruise. From the start, Cheatom did everything from sweeping decks to donning scuba gear so he could clean the undersides of the glass-bottom boats.

A graduate of Ocala High School, Cheatom married his high school sweetheart in 1959. Having grown up on a farm, Betty Cheatom said she had no problem with her husband handling gators and other wild critters.

"Whatever makes him happy makes me happy," she said. "As long as he doesn't mention snakes to me, I'm fine. I have a horror of snakes. It don't have to be more than two inches long."

The Cheatoms still live in the house Tooey gave them as a wedding gift, along with two property lots, just one mile from Silver Springs. For Cheatom, it was a short jaunt to his daily job, where, in 1979, he became manager of Wild Waters, which was then only a year old. He held that position for five years, then returned to Silver Springs as supervisor of wildlife.

Over the years, Cheatom set up underwater props for film crews, drove passenger boats, handled reptiles alongside the park's herpetologist Ross Allen and, as a deputy for the Sheriff's Office, patrolled the river on weekends and holidays.

Cheatom's claim to fame was his stunt work driving a high-speed boat in *Smokey and the Bandit III*, and he also appeared on the cover of a June 1971 *Popular Mechanics* magazine while demonstrating a two-man underwater submarine that sold as a kit for $400.

For Cheatom, a high point was when he planted rye, corn and Bahia grass to feed the area's wildlife. A low point was the fire that raged through the park in 1955. "All the buildings were burned. The only thing that was left was the glass-bottom boats," Cheatom recalled. "The park was closed for only one day. Buck Ray had people from the community come in and set up makeshift buildings, and we were open the whole time while they were building it back."

During his career, Cheatom watched Silver Springs go from a nature preserve to a theme park, with multiple management changes and a variety of man-made attractions brought in. Despite a failed attempt to return the park to a more natural setting in 1975, crowd-luring attractions increased with each change of hands. Florida Leisure introduced the Jeep Safari, the Lost River Voyage, "A Touch of Garlits" auto museum and a white alligator exhibit. In 1996, Ogden Entertainment added several rides, shows, exhibits and eateries.

"What killed Silver Springs was too many times being sold, and too many managers," Cheatom said. "When Palace Entertainment came in, I could tell they weren't really interested in Silver Springs. They were interested in making money. We had had the same spiel on our boats for years, and they came in and said we weren't talking right. They brought in a professional to teach us how to talk and changed everything around. They even changed the names of every spring we had. What used to be the Reception Hall, the Bridal Chamber and the Christmas Tree Springs got names like the Abyss and the Snowstorm Springs."

Marion County Sheriff Capt. Leon Cheatom talks about his lifelong career at Silver Springs at the Sheriff's Work Camp in Ocala, FL on Tuesday June 25, 2013. He has several scrap books that show the many things he participated on. This page shows him underwater with an alligator. Cheatom started at the springs at 14 and did every job there until the latest owner laid him off several years ago. (Alan Youngblood/OCALA STAR-BANNER) 2013

With the upcoming takeover by the state on Oct. 1, the park will go full circle, back to being a nature preserve.

To Cheatom, it's long overdue.

"I'm all for going back to nature, but they're going to have to have some kind of entertainment value in order to get the guests," Cheatom said. "I don't have any problem with them getting rid of the exotic animals. I think that's the best thing they've ever done. But if they're going to do that, they need to start feeding the native wildlife, the turkeys and the deer. The jeep trail's got a good surface. They could make that one of the best nature walks there is."

Cheatom said he's only been back to the park once since he left.

"I just walked in and stood on the main walkway and looked around," he said. "I didn't cry, but I wanted to. It was so heartbreaking to see nobody's taking care of things. For 55 years, I put in a lot of time on that river keeping it up for the guests to see. I've seen it in its heyday, and I've never seen it so low down. It really hurt."

SILVER SPRINGS—THE NEXT 50 YEARS?

Robert L. Knight, Ph.D., Howard T. Odum Florida Springs Institute
(Reprinted from the Gainesville Sun, September 2008)

I first visited Silver Springs in August 1953. I was only five years old and little did I know that a three-year landmark ecological study was underway under the direction of a new, young professor at the University of Florida named Howard T. Odum. I remember the crystal clear waters, giant catfish, and beautiful underwater "grasses." I took away an almost dreamlike memory of Silver Springs that has stayed with me since that day.

Fast forward to my last undergraduate semester at the University of North Carolina, during the spring of 1970. On the advice of a friend I signed up for Systems Ecology being taught by the same Dr. H.T. Odum. The course inspired me to pursue a career in environmental science and aquatic ecology. I also had my first exposure to Dr. Odum's acclaimed work at Silver Springs from the 1950s, a 57-page monograph that was known worldwide as one of the most complete and intuitive descriptions of any aquatic ecosystem in the world. I learned that the Silver Springs that I remembered from my childhood was renowned in science and as a tourist attraction that was synonymous with sunny Florida.

Following completion of my Master's degree and four years of research in stream ecology I renewed my contact with Dr. Odum and came to the University of Florida to earn a doctorate degree. In his most famous publication, Dr. Odum noted how constant Silver Springs had been throughout recorded history (about 100 years) and probably over the past 10,000-plus years that people had lived next to the springs. This consistency of extremely high flow (nearly 600 million gallons per day), water clarity unrivaled in any other natural aquatic environment in the world, has resulted in a diverse and productive biota.

I couldn't have been more excited when Dr. Odum suggested I restudy Silver Springs, with the intention of repeating many of the measures he had made about 25 years previously. In his seven years back in Florida he had already seen that Silver Springs was changing. My two years of graduate research found that this giant of springs was still highly productive and relatively resilient to the more intensely developed surroundings. But disturbingly I also found that the fish community at Silver Springs had declined by 78 percent during the intervening 25 years and the changes were linked in time to the construction of Rodman Reservoir downstream on the Ocklawaha River.

Much later in my career I once again was offered a chance to work at Silver Springs. With funding from the Florida Springs Initiative and collaboration with the St. Johns River Water Management District and UF faculty I spent another year (2004-2005) conducting field work and helped prepare a 50-year retrospective evaluation of the ecological health of Silver Springs. What I saw in the springs and what our data showed was alarming and did not bode well for Silver Springs' future. Fish populations had continued to decline (an estimated 92 percent reduction in their biomass over 50 years), nitrate nitrogen concentrations had increased by 200 percent, great masses of filamentous algae were now covering the sand and limerock bottom, flows were lower, water clarity had declined, dissolved oxygen in the river was lower, and overall ecosystem productivity was reduced by 27 percent. All of the old timers I spoke to at Silver Springs had been lamenting visible changes for years. Now the impacted conditions in the spring were confirmed with scientific data.

The Silver Springs Retrospective Study also forecast the condition of Silver Springs 50 years in the future (2055) as a result of continuing development in Marion County. These estimates predict an additional 84 percent increase of nitrate concentrations, an 18 percent additional decrease in flows, and further degradation of the biological community in Silver Springs.

The three Silver Springs studies described above ended with numerous conclusions and recommendations, one of which was to continue to collect more quantitative ecological data in order to track the changing health of this complex and unique ecosystem. Even more importantly, these studies found that immediate action needed to be taken to stop the rate of decline of this living masterpiece while knowledge caught up. Those recommended emergency actions include the adoption of local land use restrictions in the immediate springshed to reverse the alarming trends of increasing nitrates in the spring, re-evaluation of permitted consumptive water uses in the vicinity of the spring to preserve spring inflows from the aquifer, and accelerated evaluations of removing the Kirkpatrick Dam downstream on the Ocklawaha River to re-enable the free passage of fish and aquatic wildlife such as manatees between Silver Springs, the St. Johns River, and the Atlantic Ocean.

Most of us have experienced an utter sense of frustration upon entering an emergency room in a hospital with what we think is a serious injury and with the apparent inaction of the staff. That has been my feeling over the past two years since this report was published. Some may not think that there is enough science to move forward with actions critically needed to begin to restore Silver Springs to its previously pristine condition. Do we really know that the social costs of land use changes such as reduced fertilizer use, restricted wastewater disposal practices, capping of consumptive uses, and restoration of a prime fishing lake are really worth an attempt to

Okahumkee River Boat leaving Silver Springs, 1880s (Florida Archives).

save the life of this spring? What if we rush to make those changes and find that we have not returned Silver Springs to its former state of near perfection? Should we wait until there is more science, more people living and recreating near and in the spring, and more degradation?

Sometimes when we have to make a difficult and possibly expensive medical decision concerning our own health, we may be tempted to gather more evidence of the severity of the condition and putting off treatment or major lifestyle changes. But when that patient is our child or other loved one and the possible consequence of inaction is permanent disability or death, we are not likely to wait for more evidence when there are obvious remedies we can start taking to avoid disaster.

Silver Springs is a dream of unspoiled nature to hundreds of thousands of people, in Florida and throughout the entire world. Are we really going to take a wait-and-see approach to curing and ultimately protecting this loved one?

SILVER SPRINGS PHOTOGRAPHER BRUCE MOZERT BLAZED UNDERWATER TRAILS

Story by Marian Rizzo/ Correspondent

(Reprinted from the July 11, 2013, article in the Ocala Star-Banner Newspaper)

Photographer Bruce Mozert sat in his Ocala studio recently and reminisced over photos scattered across his desks and covering the walls like wallpaper. At 96, Mozert's lined face brightened as he spoke about his 30-year career as Silver Springs' official photographer and the unconventional methods for which he became known.

One of the highlights of Mozert's career was his design of an underwater camera housing that he made out of sheet metal, soldering wire, Plexiglas

Bruce Mozert, 96, talks about his career as the Silver Springs photographer and film maker as his Silver Springs, Fl studio on Tuesday July 2, 2013. Mozert pioneered underwater photography and built his own camera housings. He also invented filter systems to accurately shoot underwater in color. (Alan Youngblood/OCALA STAR-BANNER)2013

and a few nails and screws. Mozert first made the waterproof box-shaped casing in the 1930s, while visiting Silver Springs during the filming of the *Tarzan* movies. "I saw that crystal clear water and that's how I got into my underwater work," said Mozert, who also planned to shoot photos of the stars who were coming to Silver Springs.

His underwater housing, however, needed one more part to make it complete. "I went out in the backyard of Silver Springs one morning after I had made the camera case and I found an old inner tube," Mozert recalled. "That was back when they were made out of real rubber. I fitted it on my arm and my arm fit tight. I attached it to the housing and took it down in the water. Johnny Weissmuller was there. They all laughed at me, but all 12 pictures came out clear. They ended up sending them to Hollywood."

Mozert later designed another housing to accommodate a movie camera and created an underwater electronic strobe light system.

Named by divephotoguide.com as being among the pioneers of underwater photography, Mozert is listed along with William Thompson, who took the first underwater pictures in 1856, and Frenchman Louis Boutan, whose photo of a hardhat diver was the first underwater photo ever published.

As for his subject matter, Mozert never settled for the mundane. While shooting an ad for Mercury Marine, he arranged for a cabin cruiser to be hoisted into his backyard swimming pool. At Silver Springs, he posed attractive models in the main spring with a variety of weighted props, including kitchen stoves, lawnmowers and bathtubs. He posed his subjects shooting arrows at targets, playing golf, eating a picnic lunch and toying with fish.

If something didn't work, he found a substitute. A couple of Alka-Seltzer tablets gave the impression of bubbles ascending from a champagne glass. A splash of evaporated milk resembled smoke rising from a barbecue grill.

While Mozert was taking underwater photos for a Burma Shave commercial, the shaving cream dissolved before he could take the picture. To Mozert, it was no problem.

"Ricou (Browning) came down with a beard on," Mozert recalled. "I said, 'Go up to the shop and get some cold cream.' He smeared that on and the photo went into a national ad."

Sometimes Mozert even manipulated wildlife for the sake of a photo. Using a trail of peanuts, he lured a squirrel to look through a pair of eyeglasses at a book.

Then, there was "Big John, the talking bass" that moved too fast for a still shot. "We'd hold him out of the water long enough to get him tired, then we'd leave him go and he'd swim nice and slow and we'd get lots of pictures," Mozert said.

$$\sim$$

Mozert stumbled into the world of photography at a young age. Born Robert Bruce Mozert on Nov. 24, 1916, in Newark, Ohio, he moved with his family to a chicken farm in Scranton, Pa., while he was a youngster. After graduating from high school, he drove a coal truck. But, after only a couple runs, he accepted an invitation from his sister Zoe to move to New York City. Zoe, a professional model, introduced young Bruce to noted *Life Magazine* photographer Victor DePalma, who hired Bruce as a film developer for $3 a week. Within a year, Mozert was shooting his own pictures.

"I took to it like a duck to water," Mozert said. "Then, I started working for Black Star (photo agency) and got some odd-ball jobs. I got a whole front cover of a painter painting the Williamsburg Bridge. I didn't have any sense back then. I went out on those cables over the Hudson River and took the pictures. The daring things I did was how I got ahead so fast."

In 1938, Mozert was on his way to Miami to complete a photo history of ladies' shoes. During a stop in St. Augustine, he heard that a film crew was making *Tarzan* movies at Silver Springs. He dropped everything, came to Ocala and got a job there. Except for a brief stint in the Air Force, where he learned aerial photography, Mozert was Silver Springs' official photographer for more than 30 years. He also opened his own shop nearby and did a variety of picture-taking on land, under the sea and in the air.

Evelyn Yorlano, Mozert's office manager for 36 years, said she'll never forget when Mozert took her up in his Cessna 182 Skylane so he could take aerial photographs of Marion County.

"He was letting go of the controls and reaching in the back seat for his camera," she said. "While he was hanging out of the plane, I was holding the steering wheel. If he said tip it, I tipped it. With one hand, I'm holding the controls. With the other hand, I'm holding onto his belt."

During Mozert's career at Silver Springs, he shot photos of such notables as Gregory Peck, Jane Wyman, Lloyd Bridges and Richard Egan.

"The photos I shot of Jayne Mansfield went worldwide," Mozert said. "She was nobody until she came to Silver Springs and boy did she play up the photography."

For his underwater work, Mozert often shot professional models with a variety of props. Among his "pin-up girls" was Ginger Stanley (now Hallowell), who also was a stunt swimmer for the first two *Creature from the Black Lagoon* movies. Hallowell, now of Orlando, recalled how Mozert set up the scenes for visiting movie companies.

"He would go down before they ever got there and take still photographs of every scene," Hallowell said.

They also teamed up for numerous advertisements.

"Mostly, it was doing things underwater that were usually done on land—a circus, a fashion show, a beauty contest, a picnic," Hallowell said. "We would hold our breath and go down and spread the picnic cloth and all the things that went on it, all we could do on a breath of air. Then, we would come up and take another breath. We did it frame-by-frame. It would appear as if we did it all at one time but, actually, we would be down there for an entire day to get one minute of film."

After Hallowell left to be married, Ocalan Betty Frazee (now Haskins) worked at Silver Springs from 1957 to 1960. A beauty pageant queen, she also did stunt swimming for the *Sea Hunt* series and several movies, including Jerry Lewis' *Don't Give Up the Ship*.

"Bruce just told me what to do and I did it," Haskins said. "We had tons of funny experiences. He had me eating a banana underwater. I drank a Coke, and I smoked a fake cigarette. Another time, they had a wrestling match underwater. The wrestlers were two big, burly guys, Vernon Arnette and Lee Popple, and I was the underwater referee. I wore a striped outfit. It actually made *Parade Magazine*."

A few years ago, Mozert's unique style caught the eye of Gary Monroe, a professor of fine arts and photography at Daytona State College and author of the University Press of Florida book "Silver Springs; the Underwater Photography of Bruce Mozert."

Monroe said he was doing research for a book about the St. Johns River when he was drawn to Silver Springs and spotted Mozert's work.

"I was poking around the gift shop and saw fading 8-by-10 glossies tacked to a wall, and they were his," Monroe recalled. "I was just haunted by his amazing photographs of Silver Springs, so I went to his shop and said I would like to write a book about them. He thought I was kidding. I told him, 'I think if your photos were in Manhattan galleries, they could sell for $3,500.' He rolled off his chair in hysterics. To him, the pictures were worth one dollar. He had no idea that he had created and was sitting on a treasure trove, a cultural artifact that is invaluable to our state's cultural heritage."

Mozert and Norma, his wife of 27 years, live in Ocala. He and his first wife, the late Elizabeth Dinkins Mozert, had three sons, who are deceased. When the state takes over the park on Oct. 1, Mozert said he would like to repeat what he did years ago when he shot pictures of people on the jungle cruise and glass-bottom boats, slipped the photos in a folder and sold them for $3 each. "I'd like to have a shop in the middle and shoot color pictures with glass bottom boats in the background," he said. "When people walk back, they'll see their pictures there."

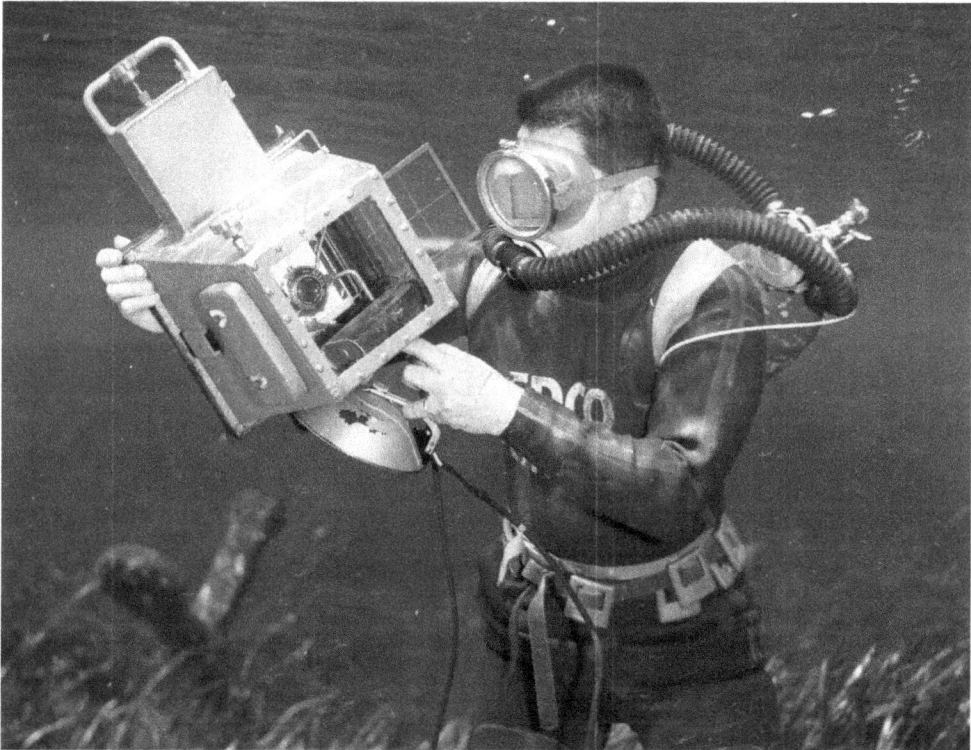

Bruce Mozert working with one of his first underwater camera housings. (Florida Archives).

HOW CAN WE SAVE FLORIDA'S ENDANGERED SPRINGS?

Robert L. Knight, Ph.D., Howard T. Odum Florida Springs Institute
(Reprinted from the Gainesville Sun, June 2012)

In the 1850s Florida's pioneers assumed that Silver Springs had always existed and would continue to flow for all eternity. Yet, Silver Springs' historic average flow (more than 500 million gallons per day (MGD) declined to about one-half of its long-term average in 2011 (247 MGD) and is currently about one-third of its long-term average flow (160 MGD). Silver Springs is literally dying before our eyes—without flow a spring becomes a stagnant sinkhole with the almost complete loss of aquatic life.

So, what causes a spring with more than 150 years of recorded history to stop flowing? There are only two possible factors that could have caused the observed flow declines at Silver Springs: a drastic reduction in rainfall and/or a drastic increase in groundwater pumping. In Marion County, rainfall has remained relatively constant, averaging about 54 inches per year over the past 96 years and 52 inches per year over the past decade. Luckily for us rainfall has not stopped. On the other hand, groundwater pumping in Marion County was non-existent 150 years ago. Today there are 931 active groundwater Consumptive Use Permits (CUPs) in Marion County for a permitted allocation of 84 MGD. This figure does not include the thousands of private self-supply wells in the county. Even more significant are the 28,630 CUPs with a combined pumping capacity of 4,700 MGD in the three water management districts that surround the groundwater basin that feeds Silver Springs. This astounding number of permits and allocated withdrawals have lowered the regional groundwater levels from coast-to-coast, resulting in reduced flow to springs and rivers, lower lake levels, and coastal salt water intrusion.

We can't control the rain. But fortunately, we can control how much groundwater we pump. There is a precedent where we have reduced our reliance on groundwater. The Tampa Bay "water wars" are a case-in-point. In the late 1980s it became increasingly obvious that groundwater pumping was lowering lake levels and drying up wetlands near Tampa. After an extended legal battle, in 1997 the Florida legislature required the opposing parties to settle their dispute and reduce their dependence on groundwater by increasing their use of surface water supplies.

The answer to the question above "How can we save our endangered springs?" is simple. Florida needs to cut back significantly on groundwater pumping. If we cannot live without that water, then we must shift to surface water supplies. The first target should be to cut back to pre-1990 pumping rates. Once we see how much that will restore flows at Silver and other imperiled springs, we may need to cut back further. These cuts need to be across the board, not only in Marion County, but from Weeki Wachee to Jacksonville and from Daytona to Tallahassee. Our "eternal" springs are dying the "death by a thousand cuts" wherever they are in Florida. And so too is our state's future.

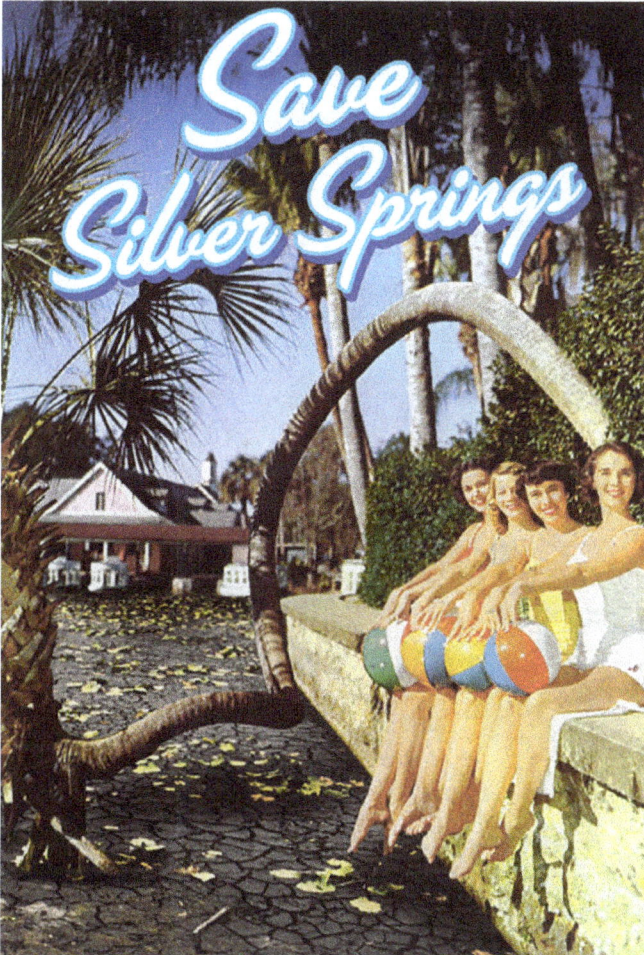

Original artwork by Rick Kilby illustrating the scary irony of a depleted Silver Springs.

A Silver Springs story:
Ricou Browning was the Creature

Story by Marian Rizzo/ Correspondent
(Reprinted from the July 18, 2013, article in the Ocala Star-Banner Newspaper)

In the mid-1950s, a grotesque costume turned Ricou Browning from a soft-spoken family man into an ugly "gill man," also known as the *Creature from the Black Lagoon*.

Now remembered along with King Kong and Godzilla as one of the most horrific monsters of the silver screen, Browning had the underwater role of the amphibious monster in the Universal Studios black-and-white horror flick, originally shot in 3-D. Browning then continued filling that role in two sequels, *Revenge of the Creature* and *The Creature Walks Among Us.*

According to Browning, the underwater portions of the film were shot at Silver Springs, Wakulla Springs and in a tank at Marineland in St. Augustine. While professional actors played the creature on land, Browning donned the full-body suit for the underwater scenes.

"It was cumbersome at first," Browning recalled.

Ricou Browning as the Creature (Florida Archives)

"When I first put it on, it seemed awkward and clumsy. But, once I got into the movie, I forgot I had it on. I became the creature."

While Browning's swimming ability made him a perfect candidate for the monster's role, his daughter, Renee Le Feuvre, who is working on her dad's biography, remembers him as a mild-mannered, but fun, family man. She recalled the exotic animals he brought home in a day when a permit for such pets wasn't required.

"Every time he got an idea for a movie, he would bring the animals home," Le Feuvre said. "We had a sea lion that sat at the dinner table. My dad wrote a movie about a sea lion called *Salty*. We had otters, a baby black bear, and a female peacock that would sit on our shoulder and drink iced tea out of our glass. All the kids in the neighborhood wanted to come over to our house, because it was like a zoo."

Browning, born Feb. 16, 1930, in Fort Pierce, was like most other Florida-bred youngsters who gravitated to the water early in life. While in the Air Force, he swam on the military swim team.

But, years before that, as a teenager, he hooked up with Newt Perry, best known for his stand-in performance for Johnny Weissmuller. Perry did the swim scenes in the *Tarzan* films that were shot at Silver Springs in the late 1960s.

When Perry opened Weeki Wachee Springs, Browning worked there as a lifeguard and also swam in the water shows. While there, Browning learned an underwater hose-breathing technique Perry had taught the mermaids. Browning later used that same technique for the "Creature" films.

"I learned to breathe from the end of an air hose," Browning said. "It was like if you're in the backyard and have a hose running. You drink what you want and let the rest spill out."

Though Browning has been clocked holding his breath for up to four minutes, he modestly denied it was a regular ability.

"If you're not doing anything at all, four minutes is possible, but not if you're moving in the water," he said. "If you're swimming fast or fighting, you use up a lot of oxygen, and it cuts it down to, at the most, two minutes."

Browning dove head-first into the film industry. Over the years, he worked as a second unit director, underwater sequence director and stunt coordinator. Some of Browning's film work also took him to the Bahamas, where he coordinated the underwater segments for *Thunderball*, was a technical adviser for Mike Nichol's *Day of the Dolphin* and directed a Lloyd Bridges special, *Man Against the Sea.*

He also was a stuntman in two dozen films, a dozen of which were shot at Silver Springs, including *Don't Give Up the Ship, Hello Down There* and the James Bond feature *Never Say Never Again.* Browning said he also participated in 30 episodes of *Sea Hunt.*

"I played all the bad guys in *Sea Hunt,*" he said.

"Courtney Brown doubled for Lloyd Bridges," Browning added, in reference to a former swim buddy who lived in Ocala during the filming and died in Pompano Beach in 2007.

Browning worked closely with several other Ocalans at Silver Springs. Among them were Bill Ray, Bruce Mozert, Pat Nelson, Bud and Patsie Boyette, and the Silver Springs mermaids, Betty Frazee and Ginger Stanley, who also was a swim double for Julie Adams in *Creature from the Black Lagoon.*

Browning also collaborated with his sister's husband, Jack Cowden, in a couple of writing projects, giving movie-goers the family films *Salty* and *Flipper,* which also became a TV series.

Browning said the idea for *Flipper* came to him after he and Newt

Ricou Browning as the Creature carrying off Ginger Stanley (Florida Archives)

Perry traveled to South America and captured fresh-water dolphins in the Amazon River.

"We brought them back to Silver Springs," Browning said. "I became their parent, apparently, and took care of them. One day, when I came home, the kids were watching *Lassie* on TV, and it just dawned on me, 'Why not do a film about a boy and a dolphin?' I was a slow writer and Jack was a great writer, so I got with him. We went to Bruce Mozert's cabin on the lake, spent a weekend there and wrote the story."

After several failed attempts to find a publisher for their book, Browning contacted *Sea Hunt* creator, Ivan Tors, whom he had met while working on the TV series.

"Ivan liked it and got with MGM," Browning said.

Today, at 83, Browning lives near Fort Lauderdale with his wife, Fran. He said he sometimes returns to Ocala to visit friends. Though it's been years since any major filming has been done at Silver Springs, Browning said the park's best feature, its crystal clear water, could still attract the movie moguls.

"I think it's possible," he said. "I think it has as much to do with the people who run it and how well they cooperate with the people that want to film. For the Creature, they didn't do any topside filming. They only shot underwater. As far as underwater activity is concerned, it hasn't changed. Except for a little more grass, it's still the same."

"FIRST, DO NO HARM"

Robert L. Knight, Ph.D., Howard T. Odum Florida Springs Institute
(Reprinted from the Gainesville Sun, September 2012)

"Primum non nocere" (first, do no harm) is commonly referred to as the Hippocratic Oath, the pledge taken by all physicians. Perhaps this oath should also be taken by public servants responsible for the health of Florida's environment.

The absence of normal rainfall in North Central Florida earlier this year revealed an inconvenient truth—there is not enough water left in the aquifer during dry spells to maintain the baseflow of our springs. As long as we have average rainfall, the springs keep flowing and it is easier to believe that long-term flow declines in our springs are just a response to a low spot in a multi-decadal weather cycle. But strip away normal rain and what is left? In May of 2012 prior to the onset of the rainy season, Silver and Rainbow springs in Marion County had the lowest flows ever recorded in more than 80 years. Over the past 25 years the average flows from Silver Springs have been declining at a precipitous rate. While last year's drought was one cause for these extreme flow declines, there is convincing evidence that excessive groundwater pumping has made a bad situation worse.

Due to Marion County's limestone geology, the underground basins or springsheds that recharge groundwater to Silver and Rainbow Springs are adjacent and overlap. Flows at both Silver and Rainbow Springs have been declining in magnitude for the past sixty years. Silver and Rainbow flow trends were roughly parallel for the first 35 years of this period. From 1950 to 1985, Silver's flow averaged about 495 million gallons per day or on average about 51 MGD higher than Rainbow's flow.

Beginning in 1985, Silver Springs' average annual flow began to decline at a faster rate than the flow at Rainbow Springs. As a consequence of this accelerated flow decline, Silver Springs lost its dominance over Rainbow

Springs in 1998. Since that time Rainbow Springs has had higher annual average flows than Silver Springs in all years, averaging about 76 million gallons per day higher in 2011. Since 2000 there has been a long-term average flow reduction of at least 32% at Silver Springs and 18% at Rainbow Springs. Combined, the two springs have lost more than 200 million gallons per day and have lower flows now than at any time in recorded history. This in spite of the fact that annual rainfall totals over the past decade in Marion County are still within the range of rainfall totals recorded over the past 100 years.

These data indicate that there is something very wrong in the springsheds that feed these two first magnitude artesian springs. One plausible explanation was offered by water management district hydrologists in 2010. The groundwater-divide that formerly marked the intersection between the Silver and Rainbow springsheds was not apparent on regional groundwater level maps during dry years as early as 1985. Since Rainbow Springs' water surface is about 12 feet lower than the water surface at Silver Springs, it was suggested by District staff that Rainbow Springs might be "pirating" flow from Silver Springs during dry periods. This hypothesis suggests that the groundwater basin feeding Silver Springs has diminished in size relative to the springshed that feeds Rainbow Springs. Movement of the groundwater divide between the two springsheds can occur due to a combination of groundwater pumping and reduced recharge of rainfall.

A second plausible explanation for the observed spring flow declines is a regional lowering of the surface of the Floridan Aquifer due to a combination of lower rainfall and increased groundwater pumping. The U.S. Geological Survey, the Florida Geological Survey, and the St. Johns and Southwest Florida Water Management Districts have all documented regional aquifer declines in North and Central Florida over the past 40-plus years. Lower aquifer levels equate to lower spring flows. The key question is: what is the principal cause of these aquifer declines—less rainfall or more pumping?

In May 2012 the Florida Springs Institute brought the accelerating declines in flow at Rainbow and Silver Springs to the attention of the Secretary of the Florida Department of Environmental Protection and to the governing boards of the two responsible water management districts. The response by these state agencies was encouraging since they pledged to work together to develop a thorough understanding of what was happening to the flows at these two first magnitude springs. The agencies began sharing and comparing rainfall, aquifer level, and spring flow data in July 2012 and developed their preliminary findings for public announcement in late August 2012. In summary they concluded that:

- There is a strong decline in both cumulative rainfall and cumulative spring flow at Silver and Rainbow Springs over the past fifty years, illustrating the significance of rainfall to maintain spring flow.
- Water management district models indicate that existing estimated human groundwater withdrawals account for approximately 1 percent of the long-term average flow reduction observed at Rainbow Springs and about 5 percent at Silver Springs. The majority of spring flow change at Rainbow is due to changes in rainfall. Increased vegetation growth in the Silver River has resulted in an additional flow reduction at Silver Springs of about 67 million gallons per day (about 13 percent of the historic average flow).
- The springshed boundaries between Rainbow and Silver Springs naturally move in response to rainfall variations and there is little evidence to suggest permanent shifts in their boundaries.

These findings and explanations are unsatisfactory for at least two reasons. First, they assign responsibility for declining spring flows to natural phenomena that are largely beyond human control, and then do not require reduced groundwater pumping to help offset the hypothesized effects of naturally low rainfall and recharge. Second, they ignore the fact that groundwater pumping from the same aquifer that feeds these two springs has increased exponentially throughout North and Central Florida since the 1930s. Human groundwater withdrawals from the Floridan Aquifer were virtually non-existent in the 1930s and have swelled to over 2.6 billion gallons per day in 2010.

The simple facts are:

- The Upper Floridan Aquifer is a single unit extending for hundreds of miles north and south of these springs.
- Groundwater extractions that occur anywhere in the Floridan Aquifer have an effect on water levels everywhere in the aquifer.
- Before pumping began in the early 20th century, most rainfall and runoff that recharged the aquifer discharged as flows to spring runs

and rivers at an estimated rate of about 10 billion gallons per day.
- Current groundwater pumping is more than 25 percent of the estimated pre-development spring flow.

The inevitable logic of these basic hydrogeologic truths is that all groundwater pumping has a negative effect on spring flows. The evidence is that nearly all of the 1,000-plus springs in Florida that have been monitored have flow reductions, and a number of springs have ceased to flow all together. The challenge for wise groundwater management is to accurately estimate the proportion of this observed flow reduction that can be controlled by a society that wishes to preserve the integrity and the multitude of biological and economic services that springs provide. In the never-ending absence of certainty about the spring flow loss attributable to pumping, a thoughtful water manager should err on the side of conserving the resource rather than continuing to increase permitted groundwater withdrawals.

Lowering of aquifer levels and the possible movement of the groundwater divide in Marion County is symptomatic of a regional failure by water management districts to use necessary precaution during allocation of groundwater resources. The age-old principal of "Primum non nocere" (First, Do No Harm) dictates preserving the life of the patient rather than subjecting him or her to additional unintentional damage. Over-exploitation of the Floridan Aquifer within and outside of Marion County is likely resulting in the unintentional transfer of millions of gallons per day of groundwater flow away from Silver Springs and the St. Johns River and towards the Rainbow River and the Gulf of Mexico. More tangible to the public interest is the fact that the lifeblood of Silver and Rainbow springs is not being protected during droughts, but rather is being squandered to irrigate lawns in one of the wettest regions in the United States.

Wise management of surface and groundwater in Florida is the state's responsibility. Water resource decisions by law must be in the public's best interest, be reasonable and beneficial, and must not impact other legal uses. Florida's water is the state's "commons," a natural resource to be conserved for the lasting benefit of all future generations. Nevertheless, Consumptive Use Permits are issued by the State's water management districts to many private, for-profit enterprises, including farms, mines, electric generating companies, golf courses, and beverage companies. Consumptive Use Permits are also issued to public utilities that supply water for public use. In total there are more than 28,000 existing Consumptive Use Permits in North and Central Florida that authorize the extraction of up to 4.6 billion gallons per day from the Floridan Aquifer. Another million or more domestic self-supply wells also pump water from the underground aquifer.

Florida's natural environment also needs water to survive. The majority of rainfall is needed to nourish more than 30 million acres of streams, lakes, fields, and forests. Research funded by the water management districts has found that significant harm typically occurs to the ecology of springs, rivers, lakes, and wetlands with as little as a 10 to 15 percent reduction in average water levels or flows. Under natural droughts these water resources have even lower flows and levels and are more susceptible to reductions caused by human groundwater uses. Thus, in equitably dividing up Florida's water pie, it is essential to preserve more than 85 to 90 percent of the water for the natural systems.

Florida's groundwater is neither unlimited nor inexhaustible. Yet, that is the way the resource is currently managed. There is no defined allocation of groundwater between humans and nature. Responsible management to prevent environmental harm dictates quantification of a sustainable water use that first provides enough water to meet the needs of the natural environment and long-term protection of aquifer levels, with only the remainder allocated to human needs. Any other strategy is doomed to over exploitation, declining aquifer levels, and continuing degradation of water resources.

With continued groundwater pumping at current rates it is unlikely that the historic sustained flows at Silver or Rainbow springs can be restored, even if future

1950's postcard welcoming tourists to Silver Springs (Florida Archives).

rainfall totals surpass historic values. Rates of groundwater extraction need to be reduced throughout the entire Floridan Aquifer. No new groundwater Consumptive Use Permits should be issued until water managers and the public agree on a level of use that protects our springs and aquifer.

HISTORY OF UNDERWATER INNOVATION STAYS IN THE FAMILY

Story by Marian Rizzo/ Correspondent
(Reprinted from the July 27, 2013, article in the Ocala Star-Banner Newspaper)

For many folks, the name Jordan Klein conjures up images of underwater cinematography, waterproof cameras, improved scuba gear and high pressure compressors.

Jordan Klein Sr., who spent a good portion of his life beneath the sea, used his love of diving and his creativity to design and build devices that would impact the motion picture industry. Klein's projects took him from Miami to the Bahamas, and ultimately, to the waters of Silver Springs.

Jordy Klein and his father Jordan Klein talk about the equipment he is currently using including multi rotor radio controlled aircraft and high resolution digital video cameras. The Kleins have filmed for decades underwater and above water and are shown on Tuesday July 23, 2013 at their studio in Summerfield, FL. The Klein's have filmed major motion pictures, television and other films in Silver Springs and around the world. (Alan Youngblood/OCALA STAR-BANNER) 2013

Driven by his own interest in scuba diving, Klein continuously sought ways to make scuba gear safer. He also did several designs for underwater camera housings for both still and moving pictures.

In Klein's Summerfield home office, numerous trophies and framed certificates speak of his accomplishments in the field of underwater photography. Among his most notable honors are his induction into the International Scuba Diving Hall of Fame, several International Underwater Film Festival awards and a 2002 Academy of Motion Picture Arts and Sciences award for technical achievement.

At 87, Klein acknowledges his many accolades with a shrug of his shoulders and a modest twinkle in his eye. But his face lights up and his voice becomes more animated when he talks about growing up in Miami, where, at the age of 14, he piloted an airplane solo and designed his own underwater diving gear. He made fins out of a piece of a tire and two tennis shoes, and he made a face mask from a section of an inner tube and a piece of glass.

"That's what we used to dive with in the '30s and '40s," he said, adding that he and a friend also made their own diver's hard hat.

"We took a 5-gallon milk can, cut off the top and used a refrigerator compressor to pump air from the surface through a garden hose. We didn't realize we needed a non-return valve. If the hose broke, it would have collapsed our lungs and killed us," he said.

Those early attempts eventually evolved into more professionally-designed creations. In 1948, Klein bought some surplus air compressors and redesigned them to make the first Mako breathing compressors. Around the same time, he began designing underwater camera housings. And, he patented the first mass-produced "waterproof camera," the Mako Shark, which takes 120 size film and can still be used today.

Klein operated his Mako compressor company in Miami for 30 years, then moved it to Ocala in the late 1970s. The founder of Jordan Klein Productions, he said he was drawn here by his interest in the film crews that were shooting at Silver Springs.

As an underwater set designer and cameraman, Klein worked on several TV series, including *Flipper, The $6 Million Man* and *The Bionic Woman*. He also joined up with Miami producer Ivan Tors for the filming of 24 episodes of *Sea Hunt*, shot at Silver Springs, plus several major motion pictures, including two James Bond movies, *Thunderball*, which was filmed in Miami and Nassau, and *Never Say Never Again*, which was filmed in Freeport, High Springs and Silver Springs.

"I was a part-time underwater cameraman and I worked full-time taking care of the props that I built," Klein said. "I constructed the underwater bomb carriers for both James Bond films and I designed 12 electric-powered underwater scooters for *Thunderball*. The door slid open at the side of the ship and the scooters came rushing out."

Klein's son, Jordy, was a baby when his dad was working on *Thunderball*. To the younger Klein, it seemed only natural that he follow in his father's footsteps. "I lived with it every day," Jordy said. "I learned how to dive when I was 2½. My dad made a special scuba apparatus for me. He took a mouthpiece made for an adult and cut it down to fit my mouth. I started in our swimming pool. Then, he took me to the reef somewhere around the Keys."

During his high school years, Jordy worked at his father's compressor shop. He was introduced to the world of undersea film photography early in life, first by filling scuba tanks for the actors and later by doubling as a swim stand-in for the lead actor in the *Salty* movie. He also was a swim-double for Ron Ely, who had the lead of Mike Nelson in the second TV series of *Sea Hunt*.

Jordy, the owner and president of Jordan Klein Film and Video, soon transferred his interest behind the camera. As a design engineer, he also designed his own underwater camera housings and equipped a catamaran with a tower and side wings that serve as a photographer's perch over the water. For his contributions, Jordy was nominated in 2004 for a Sci-Tech award by the Academy of Motion Picture Arts and Sciences.

Jordy, also an aerial photographer, recently invented a radio-controlled helicopter with six rotors and a camera. It would be useful in agriculture, cell phone tower inspections, border patrol and traffic monitoring, Jordy said. "We've actually used it for filming alligators in the swamp for a TV show called *Swamp People*," he said.

The Kleins' most recent film project, *Whiskers*, uses a movie script Jordan Sr. wrote about a sea lion. Pending financing, Jordy said he plans to do most of the filming in Marion County at parks and shops, as well as Lake Weir and, if possible, at Silver Springs.

Jordy's wife, Arlene, has been involved in some of her husband's film-making and has had a few moments of her own in the limelight.

A tall, willowy blond with long hair, Arlene was often type-cast as a mermaid. When the Kleins were in Nassau working on the movie *Splash*, Arlene was a swim double for Daryl Hannah. Arlene also played a mermaid in a music video by Julio Iglesias and was a mermaid in a documentary about manatees, which was shot at Rainbow Springs. The episode was part of a series, *Fabulous Animals*, and can be viewed on YouTube.

"They show a close-up of my face and I morph into a manatee," she said. "It was really kind of cool."

Arlene also posed as a mermaid for several promotional videos at Silver Springs and was a passenger in an underwater car, Rinspeed sQuba, for a commercial shot by Jordy at Silver Springs.

"I've been with Jordy since I was 17 years old," Arlene said. "It's been an adventure. I have to say, the most interesting things I've done in my life were because of being married to Jordy and being part of this cool family."

To Jordy, some of his easiest work was done at Silver Springs.

"Normally, when we film underwater, it's a pain in the neck," he said. "We've got to fly somewhere where the water is clear, and then we've got to get in a boat and hope the water won't be too rough. So, it was nice to get in a car and drive there and get right in the water. The Silver River is always clean, and it's always the same temperature, so you know what to expect. Other than when it was raining, you could shoot continuously."

After Silver Springs changed hands in the 1990s, opportunities for such projects diminished, Jordy said.

"Silver Springs has become increasingly difficult to work with, mainly because of the politics involved, the price changes and the hoops we have to jump through to shoot there," he said. "It used to be a pleasure to film there. It cost $1,000 a day and they would pull a barge up in the main spring for us, and we would have their concession people cater the crew meals. When Florida Leisure sold out, it became more difficult. Then, they charged $5,000 a day, and we couldn't bring a boat in there without permission from the Corps of Engineers and the EPA, and we had to hire a couple of off-duty deputies."

With Silver Springs going under state control this fall, the wheels of creativity have already started turning for Jordan Klein Sr.

"I would like to see a restaurant with a big window in it, where you can sit and eat and look into the springs. It would be lower than the water level," he said. "If they want to get divers in there, they could build a place to go swimming through man-made galleons and treasure boxes, and a maze of underwater artifacts. Mothers can sit and watch their kiddies and husbands swimming around and exploring. And, every morning the park could throw out a bunch of silver coins—pieces of eight—that they can take home with them. And they could give diving lessons and rent scuba equipment and turn that into a serious scuba diving center," he added.

Arlene Klein, right, looks to the surface for direction during the taping of the Rinspeed amphibious car the sQuba in the main spring at the Silver Springs attraction in Silver Springs, Fl on Monday February 5, 2008. Arlene, the wife of legendary filmmaker Jordy Klein, has starred in and done double work in underwater productions for many years. (Alan Youngblood/Star-Banner) 2008

RESTORING SILVER SPRINGS
A REGIONAL CHALLENGE

Robert L. Knight, Ph.D., Howard T. Odum Florida Springs Institute

(Reprinted from the Ocala Star Banner, December 2012)

On December 11th, the Governing Board of the St. Johns River Water Management District held the fourth and final meeting concerning their new Springs Protection Initiative. The primary topics at Tuesday's meeting were the declining water flows at Silver Springs and the causes and effects of nitrate nitrogen pollution. To any attendee who might have expected to hear what the District was planning to do to ensure protection of Silver Springs, these meetings must have been alarming.

Average flows at Silver Springs during the past decade are reduced by 32 percent compared to the average of the previous 70-plus years, and down by 50 percent during the past two years. Silver Springs is also suffering from nitrate-nitrogen concentrations more than 25 times higher than historic levels, a result of excessive fertilizer use and inadequate treatment of human and animal wastes. The once clear water, verdant plant community, and abundant fish populations at Silver Springs are now all visibly degraded and disappointing to any visitor who remembers the way the springs once were.

Sadly, during their springs meetings, the St. Johns River Water Management District made no decision to restore flows to Silver Springs. District staff continue to insist that groundwater pumping is not a significant part of the documented flow decline, and instead, claim that lower rainfall totals and other natural causes are responsible for reduced spring flows. However the District's own data show that groundwater pumping from the Floridan Aquifer exceeds 1.2 billion gallons each day, which is groundwater that otherwise would have flowed to the springs. Further, regional monitoring data show that groundwater levels have already declined by up to 60 feet in heavily-pumped areas around Tampa and Jacksonville, and aquifer levels in the vicinity of Silver Springs have declined by up to 20 feet. Studies by the U.S. Geological Survey demonstrate that regional groundwater level declines severely reduce flows, even in distant springs.

Silver Springs is not healthy and its vital signs are not improving. Yet, the outcome of the four District Springs Protection Initiative workshops was a recommendation for additional research rather than immediate corrective action for problems that have been visibly worsening at Silver Springs. While increased monitoring is certainly commendable to assess the changing health of the springs, the root causes of the impacts have been well understood for more than a decade.

Due to the interconnectedness of the Floridan Aquifer, a local solution to restore flows at Silver Springs will require regional action. The only feasible approach to restoring aquifer levels and historic flows at Silver Springs is to reduce the overall groundwater extraction District-wide.

The Florida Department of Environmental Protection has determined that the amount of nitrate entering the groundwater that feeds Silver Springs needs to be reduced by at least 79 percent to control harmful algal blooms. This difficult task will require a reduction of fertilizer use by farmers and homeowners, and upgrades to wastewater treatment/disposal systems throughout much of Marion and adjacent counties.

The community that loves Silver Springs needs to draw a line in the sand and let their state officials know that no more degradation can be tolerated. All state and local permitting decisions should be based on protecting the public's interests. A healthy environment at Silver Springs equates to a healthy local and state economy. Citizens who wish to pass a restored Silver Springs to the next generation should demand that any new permits issued must be offset by an overall decrease in groundwater pumping and a reduction in the amount of nitrogen applied to the land. Otherwise Silver Springs will continue to suffer a death by a thousand cuts.

9—Boat Landing at Crystal Clear Silver Springs Florida

(Photo: Florida Archives)

SILVER SPRINGS WAS 'ONE BIG FAMILY'

Story by Marian Rizzo/ Correspondent

(Reprinted from the August 5, 2013, article in the Ocala Star-Banner Newspaper)

From her teenage years until she retired in 1988, Peggy Ann (Mixon) Collins worked at Silver Springs park on three separate occasions and in a variety of departments, including Paradise Park and Ross Allen's reptile institute. She handled admission tickets, sold snakes, posed for photos and took pictures of visitors on the glass-bottom boats.

Though Collins left the area a couple of times to pursue a career on the stage, she kept coming back to Silver Springs, a place she had begun to call home.

Peggy Collins, 82, talks about her days at Silver Springs, performing in Las Vegas, working as a movie double and life as a single mom at her Ocklawaha, FL home on Tuesday July 30, 2013. She is shown with a painting of her in her 20's. Collins is multitalented doing everything at the springs from selling tickets to working with Ross Allen.
(Alan Youngblood/OCALA STAR-BANNER) 2013

67

"We were like one big family at the springs," Collins said. "Everybody knew each other. Everybody helped each other. They made me feel right at home, that's why I always wanted to come back."

Born on June 20, 1931, in Charleston, S.C., Collins moved with her family to Gainesville when she was 3 years old, and to Ocala when she was in the seventh grade. While attending Ocala High School, her first Silver Springs job was in the office at Paradise Park, a segregated African-American area with its own beach, animal shows and festivals.

Collins said Eddie Vereen was the manager of Paradise Park and worked under Ross Allen, founder and operator of the reptile institute. With a roll of her eyes, Collins recalled the tricks Vereen used to play on her.

"Eddie would come inside in the mornings and tie something to my desk," she said. "When I opened the door to come in, a wildcat would be hissing at me or a big old boa constrictor would be on my typewriter. I drove up one morning and saw a beautiful dog tied to a tree. I rushed up and hugged him. Eddie came up and said, 'Do you know what you are petting? That's a wolf.' After that, he would call me outside during the show and had me woolly up the wolf for the visitors."

A singer and dancer, Collins left Silver Springs for a brief period to work in Hollywood and Las Vegas and to tour with a USO troupe. In 1959, newly divorced and with a toddler in tow, Collins returned to Florida and worked at Diana Shops, a former clothing store in downtown Ocala. But, it wasn't long before Silver Springs lured her back and she took a job with Ross Allen, selling admission tickets and working in his gift shop.

"I looked at Ross Allen like another daddy," she said. "I didn't like snakes, but I had to sell 'em. You'd be surprised how many people wanted these things. Their kids wanted them for birthdays and Christmas."

Now 82, Collins recalls the special details that made Silver Springs a unique tourist attraction before Disney came to Central Florida and lured the crowds away.

"I remember Silver Springs when the water was crystal clear," she said. "We girls used to swim under the glass-bottom boats and wave at the people. The drivers would cut the motors for us."

One of Collins' favorite exhibits, the Prince of Peace, was a religious display by sculptor Paul Cunningham, who died in 1985. His hand-carvings depicting the life of Jesus Christ were arranged in individual rooms within an A-frame, church-style structure.

Other exhibits also had special significance for Collins.

"There was a tower where the Osceola statue is," she recalled. "A man was up there playing the chimes. They made a beautiful sound through the trees."

Then, there was Ross Allen's reptile institute and, on the property behind it, a Seminole Indian reservation. Collins smiled as she reminisced over pictures of Indian children posing with her son, Bill Singer.

Over the years, vendors came and went, and there were changes in park management.

"Tommy Bartlett's Deer Ranch was there. You could go in and pet the goats," Collins said. "There was an artist out on the sidewalk who would paint your picture right there. Alward's Restaurant was there, too. They were known for their pecan pies. And, there was an open fountain where you could get chips and hot dogs. My son worked there on weekends while he was in school and full time in the summer."

When the attraction reached it's zenith, the number of guests jumped to 800,000 a year. Well-known stars would come there on vacation. A touch of excitement in her voice, Collins spoke about a lunch date she had with actor George Jessel. When actress Sandy Duncan came to the park on her honeymoon, Collins was selling admission tickets. They immediately recognized each other, having performed together years before at the Silver Slipper in Las Vegas.

During the park's flourishing movie years, Collins doubled for actress Mari Aldon in *Distant Drums*, a Gary Cooper film about the Seminole Indian Wars.

The crew shot for six weeks at Silver Springs and another six weeks at Marco Island, years before it became an elite residential paradise.

"At Silver Springs, I ran through the saw grass," Collins said. "I also had a scene where they were carrying me into the dirty water. I did everything the star didn't want to do."

For her work in the film, which also included a close call with three alligators at Marco Island, Collins earned $15 a day.

Collins' moments in the limelight also included posing for a postcard shot by the park's official photographer, Bruce Mozert. For the picture, Collins donned a leopard-skin bathing suit and sat with a live leopard named Lolita.

"I had the chain wrapped around my wrist and in my hand, and the leopard got edgy," Collins said. "She moved and took me into the ditch. I got all dirty and had to go wash off. Then we got back in place and Lolita was still restless. She reached over with her mouth and grabbed my arm, just hard enough to make some red marks. Bruce said, 'That's enough. It's a wrap.'"

Such was the environment where Collins, a single mother, raised her son.

Bill Singer, now a doctor of clinical psychology in Orlando, said his life at Silver Springs provided some valuable tools for his career.

"It was a great learning environment," Singer said. "I had so much diversity from people of all races, backgrounds and ages. I was like a sponge. I just soaked it up. I grew up in a place that was like the inside of a movie. Many people came from all over the world to experience what I experienced every day. I could go pretty much everywhere I wanted, and I saw things the public never saw."

Collins and her son lived for a while in a nearby cottage owned by Ross Allen's mother. Among Singer's role models were Newt Perry and his wife, who taught him how to swim in the springs, Allen, who taught him how to

Peggy Collins, multitalented, doing everything at the springs from selling tickets to working with Ross Allen. (Alan Youngblood/OCALA STAR-BANNER) 2013

call a gator, and Mozert, who put him in the darkroom developing pictures.

"By the time I was in high school, I had my own darkroom setup in my house," Singer said. "I learned skills far beyond my age."

As for his mother, Singer had many praises.

"As beautiful as she was on the outside, her heart was even bigger," he said. "She could do things with animals that other people would not think possible. She worked hard all her life. At the springs, her biggest paycheck, I think, was $50 a week or something. But I didn't know we were financially strapped, because the people shared what they had."

BLACK CLOUDS STILL LOOM OVER SILVER SPRINGS

Robert L. Knight, Ph.D., Howard T. Odum Florida Springs Institute
(Reprinted from the Gainesville Sun, February 2013)

Silver Springs has been the subject of considerable attention for the past year. Last spring Silver Springs flows were plummeting to a record low and nitrate contamination was at an all-time high.

The proposed Adena Springs Ranch was requesting a permit to withdraw an additional 13 million gallons per day from the aquifer feeding Silver Springs and was planning to put 30,000 cattle with a manure production of about 2 million pounds per day in the spring's groundwater recharge basin.

More than 1,700 local citizens attended a Speak Up for Silver Springs rally at the Silver River State Park to hear keynote speaker and ex-Governor/Senator Bob Graham call for enforcement of existing laws to protect the quantity and quality of water at Silver Springs.

One year later Silver Springs flows are still less than one half of their historic average and nitrate concentrations are more than 30 times higher than their pre-development levels. But for the first time in years there is blue sky showing through the dark clouds swirling above Silver Springs.

In response to the public's massive opposition, Adena Springs Ranch reduced their requested groundwater extraction by 60 percent and their number of cows by 42 percent.

Even with these concessions, staff of the St. Johns River Water Management District still found the revised Adena permit request insufficient and requested a mountain of additional studies to prove that this industrial farm would not cause harm to the area's surface and ground water resources.

The District's Governing Board held four public workshops to learn more about the threats facing Silver Springs and District staff have requested a greatly increased budget for springs monitoring and protection.

The Florida Department of Environmental Protection proposed and finalized a numeric nitrate standard for Silver Springs that requires regional

72

efforts to reduce nitrogen loads to the groundwater by 79 percent. The Department kicked off public workshops that will eventually lead to finalization of a basin-wide management action plan to achieve this water quality goal at Silver Springs.

And perhaps most exciting to longtime Silver Springs observers, the Department's Parks and Recreation division rolled out an interim plan to eliminate the last private tourist attraction at Silver Springs and to replace it with a customer and environmentally-focused state park that promises to end commercial exploitation of the headspring area.

These events are all good news and may preview a bright future at Silver Springs. In a more perfect world, it would appear that Silver Springs might be on course to regain its status as the biggest and most productive spring in Florida.

But black clouds still darken and reflect the green hue of this damaged natural wonder. Continuing foul weather is still in the spring's forecast, likely for decades to come. Concerned citizens should be considering what they can do to be ready for a rough period before Silver Springs is eventually returned to its former health.

Public vigilance and a healthy share of skepticism are the best protections against the continuing degradation of Silver Springs. True restoration of Silver Springs will likely require the following regional efforts:

- A permanent reduction of existing groundwater extraction throughout north and central Florida to less than 50 percent of today's rates.
- Elimination or major reduction of all urban/suburban uses of nitrogen fertilizers.
- An incentive-based program to shift agriculture from water and nitrogen-intensive crops to managed forests.
- Upgrades to all regional wastewater treatment facilities and replacement of many septic systems by central treatment facilities.
- Restoration of the Ocklawaha River to allow unimpeded migration of fish and manatees up the Silver River; and
- An informed and energized public that has easier access to Silver Springs through the new state park and the ability to recognize and oppose threats and celebrate successes.

This is an exciting time in the long history of Silver Springs. One of the wonders of the natural world, Silver Springs has the chance to turn the corner from more than 50 years of regulatory neglect and decline, to a future of recovery and protection.

Silver Springs can serve as an allegory for all of Florida's natural wonders. Either it can go the way of the Ivory Billed Woodpecker and Carolina Parakeet or it can be returned from near extinction like the Brown Pelican and the Bald Eagle.

Arrilla Jones at underwater newsstand hawking the Saturday Evening Post in Silver Springs photo by Bruce Mozert, Florida Archives).

'HUMAN FISH' HAD A LIFE FILLED WITH AQUATIC EXPLOITS

Story by Marian Rizzo/ Correspondent
(Reprinted from the August 14, 2013, article in the Ocala Star-Banner Newspaper)

Dubbed "the human fish," Newt Perry is most often remembered for his performance as a swim double for Johnny Weissmuller, the yodeling ape-man in the *Tarzan* movies of the 1930s and '40s.

But, Perry was much more than that to people who knew him.

Perry's daughter, Delee Perry, took a break between classes at Perry's

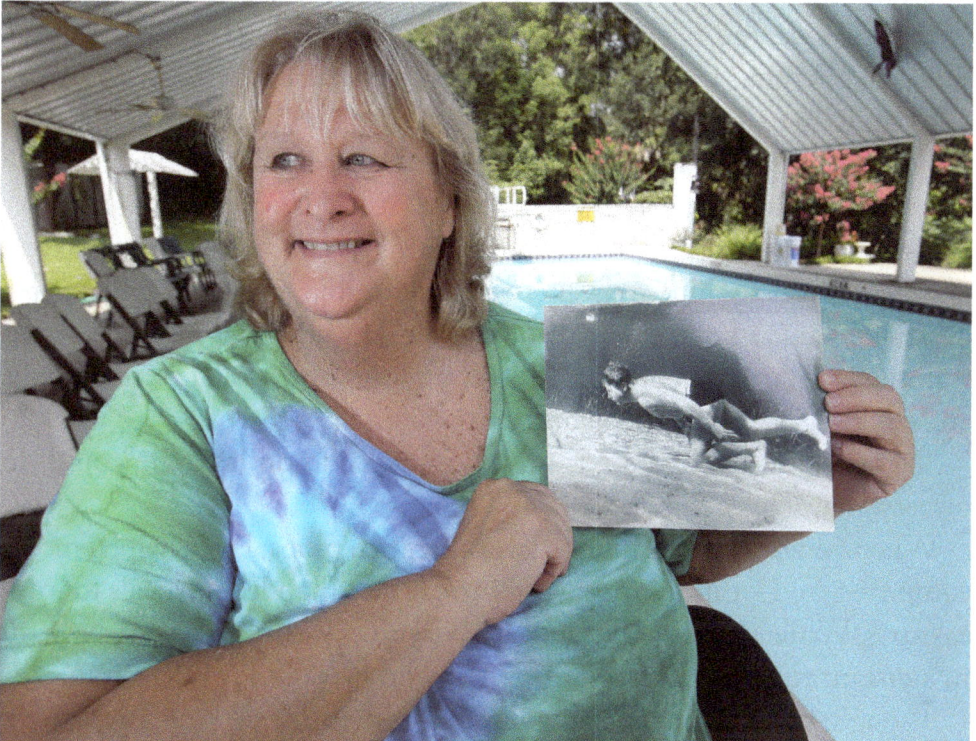

Delee Perry poses with an historic photo of her father, Newton A. Perry, at Perry's Swim School on Northeast 17th Avenue in Ocala, Fla. on Tuesday, August 6, 2013. Newt Perry was a swim stand-in for Johnny Weismuller in the Tarzan movie series. He also started Weeki Wachee and taught the mermaids how to do underwater swimming without a tank.
(Star-Banner Photo/Bruce Ackerman) 2013.

Swim School in northeast Ocala last week to talk about her father's many accomplishments.

"My dad had three jobs all my life," Delee said. "He was manager at the Ocala city pools, he taught swimming and scuba diving, and he was principal at Anthony School and Eighth Street Elementary School until he retired in 1972. And, he started Perry's Swim School in 1955."

During his career, Newt Perry taught more than 120,000 people to swim, including his nephew, Don Schollander, who won multiple gold and a silver medal in the 1964 and 1968 Olympics.

Perry also showed concern for underprivileged youth when he started a Boys Saturday Club. He bought a large truck and drove around town picking up boys to take to Silver Springs, where he taught them swimming and outdoor camping skills.

While managing Ocala's two city pools, Perry convinced local officials to offer residents two weeks of swimming lessons for $1 per person.

"My dad wanted to make swimming as financially reasonable as possible," Delee said. "He felt everybody deserved the opportunity to swim."

In addition to his role as swim double for Weissmuller, Perry doubled for Lloyd Bridges in the *Sea Hunt* TV series. He also did underwater stunts for postcards and advertisements. Photos in Delee's collection show her dad sitting at the bottom of one of the springs, running in a foot race and playing a game of Chinese checkers, all underwater. Also while underwater, he demonstrated how to fake drinking from a soda bottle and how to eat watermelons and bananas. And, he set up classrooms, picnics, nightclubs and wedding scenes in the depths of the springs.

"My dad always said anything they could do on land, he could do underwater," Delee said.

When he wasn't performing or working with props, Perry helped movie companies find locations for their films. He also rounded up locals to work as extras. While working as technical adviser for *The Yearling*, Perry brought in a distant relative, Claude Jarman III, who played Jody in the film.

Though Perry worked with some big stars, such as Ann Blyth (*Mr. Peabody and the Mermaid*) and Gary Cooper (*Distant Drums*), whenever possible he found film roles for three of his sisters, a cousin, and his daughter Delee.

"The whole family got in on this," Delee said. "If you could swim, you were doing pictures in the water. The first thing I ever did was a training film for the American Red Cross. My dad helped them set up at Silver Springs. They needed a drowning victim, and that's where I came in. I knew what a drowning person looked like, so I acted like I was drowning. All of a sudden, two rescuers came toward me. The cameraman forgot to roll. They all thought I was really drowning."

Delee's children, Tasha and Rock, also became proficient swimmers. In the movie *D.A.R.Y.L.*, Rock, the swim double for Barret Oliver, was in an aircraft seat that plunged into the water. The scene was filmed at Rainbow Springs, Delee said.

~

Newton Augustus Perry, the eldest child and only son of a railroad conductor, was born Jan. 6, 1908, in Tifton, Ga. In 1917, the family moved to Tampa, where Newt learned to swim at the age of 8. The Perrys moved to Ocala in 1922 and within a year Newt was working as a lifeguard at Silver Springs.

During high school and college, he swam with school teams that won multiple meets. In photos, he appears to be more muscular than his lean teammates. Delee said her father had a 48-inch chest that, after years of training, grew to 54 inches.

While working toward a degree in education at the University of Florida, Newt began doubling for the *Tarzan* films. At 5-foot-11 and weighing 200 pounds, and with a head full of golden curls, he made a convincing double for Weissmuller. It was during the filming of *Tarzan* that Perry developed an underwater breathing technique using an air hose and a compressor.

On a more personal note, Perry met Dorothy "Dot" Roederer in Miami where she was training for the 1948 Olympics. A tower diver and synchronized swimmer, Dot also trained with the Water Follies. On several occasions, her water ballet team performed with Esther Williams at Cypress Gardens.

Newt and Dot married in 1950 and, on Aug. 10, 1951, Delee was born. Perry was giving a swimming lesson when he got the call. He showed up at the hospital wearing wet swim trunks and flip flops.

Delee's home life had a good balance, with a no-nonsense mother and a fun-loving father.

"I had the most wonderful childhood you could imagine," Delee said.

"I think one of the things that made my dad different from my mother as an instructor was his fun and games that made it easier to learn. He would let me hold on around his neck and we would go underwater. I would try to hold my breath as long as he did. When I couldn't hold my breath anymore, I would let go and come up. Sometimes, I would go back down and drag him up."

Delee also recalled visits with her father to Silver Springs' sandy beach, which drew a crowd in the summer. She said the park staff placed three rafts in the main spring and tied them together with ropes, which also served as a boundary from the boating areas.

"The water was very cold, so we would sit on the rafts and bake in the sun," Delee said. "I had my own raft—my dad would turn over on his back in the water and I would sit on his chest, and then I would dive in," she added.

In an effort to promote swimming programs, Newt and Dot Perry developed Aquarena, an underwater attraction in Texas. They also taught swimming at Glen Springs in Gainesville, and Dot organized a water show at the Florida School for Girls (now McPherson Complex) in Ocala.

In addition to his other film work, Newt Perry participated in 80 movie shorts by Sportlight filmmaker Grantland Rice. The short films appeared with news reels and cartoons before the main features in theaters across the nation. It was Rice who first dubbed Perry the "human fish."

During World War II, when Perry was a manager at Wakulla Springs, he helped train Navy frogmen who were learning secret underwater demolition tactics. Also while at Wakulla Springs, Perry hired Ricou Browning, who would later co-write the *Flipper* TV series and would be the underwater double for the *Creature from the Black Lagoon*.

In a phone interview from his home in South Florida, Browning recalled the day Perry invited him along to check out a Central Florida property near Brooksville.

"It looked like a puddle off the side of the road," Browning said. "We walked over and here was a crystal clear spring. It was a reservoir back then. Newt leased it from St. Pete and started developing Weeki Wachee Springs. I worked there for a number of years."

Browning said Perry taught his underwater breathing technique to the Weeki Wachee swim team and mermaids. The technique, which is still used at Weeki Wachee, came in handy for the making of the *Creature from the Black Lagoon.*

Delee was about 5 years old when Browning came to Silver Springs for the filming.

"My dad originally was offered the part of the 'Creature,' but he had to turn them down because he was busy building Weeki Wachee," Delee said. "He told them, 'I've got just the guy for you,' and he recommended Ricou Browning for the part. It worked out really good."

For his unselfish dedication to sports and filmmaking, Perry received numerous honors over the years. Central Florida Community College (now the College of Central Florida) named its swimming pool for him

Newton Perry, center, is shown in an undated family photo with Johnny Weissmuller, right, during the filming of a Tarzan movie at Silver Springs, shown at Perry's Swim School on Northeast 17th Avenue in Ocala, Fla. on Friday, April 21, 2006. (Ocala Star-Banner/NYTRENG, Bruce ACK-ERMAN). Courtesy of Delee Perry. (Florida Archives)

in 1979. Perry was inducted into the Florida Sports Hall of Fame in 1981.

He has also been recognized by numerous civic groups, including the Ocala Rotary Club, the American Red Cross and the Boys Club.

"The Elks Club named him the Grand Exalted Ruler. I used to call it 'the grand poopah,'" Delee said with a laugh.

Then, in 1978, Perry suffered a mild stroke.

"He was up and walking around in two weeks," Delee said.

Five years later, a second stroke left Perry paralyzed on his left side. Sadly, Perry also lost his wife to cancer that same year.

In 1987, Perry's right leg developed septicemia and had to be amputated.

"I watched him lose the will to live," Delee recalled. "I saw him lose weight. He didn't want to go anywhere. He didn't mind people visiting, but, after awhile he would fall asleep."

Six weeks later, on Nov. 22, 1987, Newt Perry died from an aneurism. He was 79.

Newton Perry is shown in an undated family photo at Perry's Swim School on Northeast 17th Avenue in Ocala, Fla. on Friday, April 21, 2006. (Ocala Star-Banner/NYTRENG, Bruce ACKERMAN). (Photo courtesy of Delee Perry)

Ironically, Johnny Weissmuller had suffered a series of strokes and also died at the age of 79, three years earlier.

Shortly before he died, Perry shared with the Star-Banner his philosophy regarding the unexpected turn his life had taken.

"You've got to learn to let things go," he said. "Things change. You learn that."

GROUNDWATER NITRATE AND CANCER RISK
IS THERE A LINK?

Robert L. Knight, Ph.D., Howard T. Odum Florida Springs Institute
(Reprinted from the Gainesville Sun, March 2013)

In "Region at Risk" the *Gainesville Sun* spotlighted the high rates of fatal cancers in rural areas of North Florida. The conclusions of local cancer experts appear to be that rural residents do not receive adequate medical care needed to detect and treat cancers early. In a companion article, the Sun cites studies in North Carolina and Iowa that found that exposure to agricultural pesticides is a possible factor in increased prostate cancer in males, melanoma in farmer's spouses, and ovarian cancer risk in female pesticide applicators. But the professors interviewed for the Sun's story did not think that pesticides are likely to be the missing link to increased cancer risk in rural North Florida. In summary, this article pointed to rural poverty and increased tobacco use as possible correlates with higher local cancer death rates.

The President's Cancer Panel Report (2010) takes a much harder look at the effects of exposure to environmental contaminants and the incidence of cancer among farmers, their families, and migrant farm workers. These people "…are at highest risk from agricultural exposures…" both on the job and in their daily lives. In rural North Florida this population is almost totally dependent on private self-supply wells that draw groundwater from below the lands that are intensively farmed.

While the Sun article appears to conclude that pesticides are not elevated in groundwater in our area, there is one environmental contaminant that is clearly elevated in these drinking water wells—namely nitrate-nitrogen derived from fertilizers, animal wastes, and septic tanks.

Background nitrate-nitrogen concentrations throughout areas where the Floridan Aquifer underlies protected lands (for example, the Ocala National Forest) are less than 0.05 parts per million (ppm or mg/L). County-wide average nitrate concentrations in Union County are over 0.54 ppm, more than 10 times higher than the baseline aquifer levels. The average value in Suwannee County wells is 0.56 ppm, Gilchrist County's average is 0.41 ppm, and the average in Alachua County is 0.41 ppm, eight times higher than the background.

About 40 percent of the wells sampled in Gilchrist County had nitrate concentrations above 1 ppm, more than 20 times the baseline. Fanning Spring on the Suwannee River in Levy County has an average nitrate concentration above 5 ppm, or more than 100 times the background, and peak concentrations close to 10 ppm. Test wells in Suwannee and Lafayette counties associated with row crops frequently have nitrate concentrations above 30 ppm (600 times the baseline) and a few wells have been recorded at concentrations greater than 100 ppm (2,000 times the background level).

The President's Cancer Panel Report states that the "…most likely known mechanism for human cancer related to nitrate is the body's formation of N-nitroso compounds (NOC), which have been shown to cause tumors at multiple organ sites in every animal species tested…". The report goes on to say: "In humans, NOCs are suspected brain and central nervous system carcinogens," and that in an Iowa study, older women drinking water with elevated nitrate concentrations had increased risk for bladder cancers. The authors conclude that nitrate in drinking water at concentrations less than 10 ppm (the "safe" human drinking water standard) could be carcinogenic and that further research is warranted, especially since groundwater nitrate concentrations in many agricultural areas continue to increase.

The Florida Department of Environmental Protection and the U.S. Environmental Protection Agency have found that nitrate concentrations between 0.2 and 0.4 ppm cause a kind of "ecological cancer" in natural springs by promoting a proliferation of nuisance algae. However, the state's nitrate standard in groundwater continues to be 10 ppm, a value that has resulted in the wholesale loss of desirable submerged aquatic vegetation in a growing number of Florida's springs. To-date there has not been any publicized effort to look for a relationship between human consumption of groundwater contaminated by nitrate in Florida and the risk of increased cancer.

It has often been stated that "Springs are a Window into Our Aquifer" and are also like "Canaries in a Coal Mine." Perhaps those analogies are even truer than most people think. If you see celebrated nature photographer

John Moran's springs before and after photos at the Florida Museum of Natural History, you may conclude that the "cancerous" algal proliferation impairing our springs may be a fair warning of the unseen dangers to humans resulting from drinking polluted groundwater. With the documented increased risk of cancer deaths in North Florida's most rural counties, it is critical that state and federal epidemiologists look for a link between elevated nitrate concentrations in our groundwater and these high cancer rates.

Early postcard from Silver Springs — "Fisherman's Paradise" (Florida State Archives)

PARADISE PARK WAS A HAVEN FOR THE BLACK COMMUNITY

Story by Marian Rizzo/ Correspondent
(Reprinted from the August 22, 2013, article in the Ocala Star-Banner Newspaper)

On the southeast side of the Silver River, about a mile from the Silver Springs attraction, scrub pines, saw palmettos and cabbage palms hide a treasured piece of history beneath their scruffy tangle.

Underneath the sun-filtered brush lies a former resort that was popular with blacks from 1949 to 1969.

Designated "for colored people only," the property was developed by Carl Ray and W.M. "Shorty" Davidson, co-owners of Silver Springs from 1924 to 1962.

They called it Paradise Park.

While making improvements in the Silver Springs area, Ray and Davidson also took the time to create a tropical setting of palm trees, flowering azaleas and multi-colored pansies, specifically for black people who, because of segregation, were barred from the main attraction.

There was a sandy beach, a pavilion with a dance floor, a concession stand and a picnic area. Visitors played softball and other sports, and they went swimming there.

"I loved it," said Mary Carolyn Williams, wife of retired Ocala Police Chief Sam Williams. A sparkle came to her eyes as she reflected on outings there with two of her brothers.

"My dad would say, 'We're going swimming,' and we knew that meant Paradise Park," she said. "We'd be scampering about, grabbing towels, and putting on our swimsuits. At the park, we would tear out of that station wagon and start running down the hill into the water."

One of three major Florida beaches that catered to black people at that time, Paradise Park drew about 100,000 visitors annually. People came, sometimes by the busload, from as far away as New York and California.

Churches held baptisms and Easter sunrise services there. They had Easter egg hunts and, in the winter, Santa would come down the river on a glass-bottom boat, passing out fruit, nuts and candy to the children. Herpetologist Ross Allen set up an exhibit there. And, on Labor Day, there was a beauty pageant, sponsored by a local American Legion post.

In 1949, Mildred Jones of Sanford was crowned the first Miss Paradise Park.

"It was just an exciting place to go on hot summer days," Mary Williams said. "The water was cool, the beach was sandy, like the bottom of the spring. There was a platform near the deep end. We referred to it as 'the float.' It had ladders on it, and we would climb right up on the float. You would run into people who were doing the same thing."

Arizona Vereen Turner, left, and Reggie Lewis, right, reminisce about working at Paradise Park as they look over historic photos of the park at the Marion County Black History Museum in the Howard Academy in Ocala, Fla. on Thursday, August 15, 2013. The two are both relatives of Eddie Vereen, who managed the all-black park adjacent to Silver Springs beginning in 1949, when it was opened. The park closed in 1969. (Star-Banner Photo/Bruce Ackerman) 2013.

❧

Born in 1948, Williams grew up with segregation. She knew there were places she couldn't go, but she didn't question it until she was a teenager and got involved in the civil rights movement.

But, as a child, Williams played in happy innocence at Paradise Park.

"We would go down to the edge of the spring and we could see the shops and the glass-bottom boats on the other side," she said. "I was there with my family, and I didn't need anything else. We had people dancing to music and kids jumpin' in the water. We had fun. Why would we want to go somewhere else?"

From the time it opened in 1949 until two years before it closed, Paradise Park was managed by Eddie Leroy Vereen. Born in 1897, Vereen, with only an eighth-grade education, was a self-taught "jack-of-all-trades." In addition to overseeing Paradise Park's operation, he visited schools, colleges, churches and civic groups, where he passed out brochures and promoted the park.

Vereen retired at the age of 70 in 1967, and he died in 1975.

During the park's heyday, Vereen hired several family members to work there.

His son, Leroy, was a part-time driver of glass-bottom boats. Eddie's daughters, Henrietta "Chippie" Cunningham and Vivian Tillman, and his nieces, Arizona Vereen and Catherine Vereen (now Montgomery), worked in the gift shop, in the kitchen, and anywhere they were needed.

"We did everything," Montgomery said. "At that time, we only had so many people employed there. We worked from sunup to sundown, right up until the people left. Then we had all the school groups that would come down from all these different states. So we'd go down at 4 o'clock in the morning, put on the grits and have everything ready for the children when they come in."

Henry Jones, Eddie Vereen's nephew, first visited the park with his Boy Scout troop. Later, as a teenager, he became one of the lifeguards. Except for himself and two friends, Bobby Thomas and George McCants, all the lifeguards are gone now, he said.

"Newt Perry trained 12 of us as lifeguards," Jones said. "He trained us during the off-season in the wintertime. The water was 72 degrees. It was 62 degrees outside, and we had to go in the water to get warm.

"We had to learn all of the holds and come up alongside the person who was in trouble," Jones continued. "You haven't learned how to swim until you've swum with a concrete block held in front of you to prove you could save somebody."

Jones said the crowd sometimes was a bit overwhelming down by the river. "We'd blow everybody out of the water with a whistle, and then we'd go down to the bottom and feel around to see if anybody was down there," he said. "Nobody ever drowned at Paradise Park."

"And, there was no drinking allowed," Jones added. "I worked there six days a week, and there was not one incident. We never had to call the police."

At times, the park overflowed with visitors. One day, Arizona Vereen counted 30 buses in the parking lot. On another occasion, while placing stickers on automobile bumpers, Eddie Vereen's grandson, Reginald "Reggie" Lewis, counted 247 cars.

Lewis worked at the park from the time he was 4 years old, picking up bottles with his little red wagon for 50 cents a week, until he left at 19 to join the Air Force.

As a youngster, Lewis posed for an ink blotter advertisement with the message, "No Wonder I'm Smiling! I've Seen Silver Springs."

Mary Williams shows a picture from the Christmas at Paradise Park from when she was a child. She is with her big brother the late Craig Finley Sr. at the far left next to the police officer. Paradise park was a blacks only park down river from the head springs at Silver Springs.
(Alan Youngblood/OCALA STAR-BANNER) 2013

During his teens, he was a lifeguard. He also cooked hamburgers, met the boats when they came in, and helped keep the grounds clean.

"My granddaddy was very adamant about keeping the place clean," Lewis said. "If you went down to meet the boat and there was a piece of paper on the ground, he would remind you to go pick it up on the way back. Everything was spotless."

Best of all, admission to the park was free. Lewis recalled that the swim fee, 35 cents, included a towel and a picnic basket for storing clothes. The cost to ride the glass-bottom boat was $1.25, and the jungle cruise was 65 cents, he said. All day long, glass-bottom boats and jungle cruises carrying white people glided past Paradise Park. Lewis noticed the white people seemed fascinated with the black playground. From a distance, they could see the children splashing in the water, and they could hear the rousing music from the jukebox.

An historic photo of a woman at Paradise Park is shown at the Marion County Black History Museum in the Howard Academy in Ocala, Fla. on Thursday, August 15, 2013. Eddie Vereen managed the all-black park adjacent to Silver Springs beginning in 1949, when it was opened. The park closed in 1969. (Star-Banner Photo/Bruce Ackerman) 2013. (Photo reprinted by courtesy of the Black History Museum, Ocala, per Brenda Vereen, curator.)

On one occasion, one of the passengers claimed she had to use the bathroom facility. So, the boat captain docked and let her off.

"She didn't use the bathroom," Lewis said, laughing. "She was out there shakin' her bootie on the dance floor. A lot of people don't believe me when I say one of my grandfather's jobs was to keep the white people from coming in."

∾

The passing of the Civil Rights Act in 1964 brought long-awaited social reforms to black Americans, particularly in the south. But, in Ocala, the achievement also brought a sense of loss with the eventual dismantling of Paradise Park. Soon, Ross Allen began moving his reptiles to the Silver Springs area. By the time Lewis returned home from the Air Force in 1969, the park had already closed.

An historic photo of the Miss Paradise Park Pageant from the 1950s is shown at the Marion County Black History Museum in the Howard Academy in Ocala, Fla. on Thursday, August 15, 2013. Eddie Vereen managed the all-black park adjacent to Silver Springs beginning in 1949, when it was opened. The park closed in 1969. (Star-Banner Photo/Bruce Ackerman) 2013. (Photo reprinted by courtesy of the Black History Museum, Ocala, per Brenda Vereen, curator.)

"Everybody was sad, because it was like home to most of the blacks," Lewis said. "Integration was good to a point, but we also lost. It was a part of the black community. When they closed it down, it took something away from everybody."

Today, Paradise Park remains buried beneath the underbrush. However, 10 years ago, Ocala photographer Cynthia Graham set out on a quest to revive memories of the long-forgotten park. She began gathering photos and data for a book to be written through a collaboration with Lucinda Vickers, a writer in Tallahassee. Graham also visited the park with Leon Cheatom, who was employed at Silver Springs at the time.

"We got in a Jeep and drove down Paradise Road, and he took me in by foot," Graham recalled. "Then, he took me on a boat down the river to show me where the park was off the river. Everything was overgrown, and there was debris from the concrete benches. There was nothing else left. You can't get to the beach area. You can't tell there ever was a park back there."

In the beginning, Graham met with disappointment when she realized very little had been written about Paradise Park.

"What I thought would take me six months to write has taken me 10 years just to gather this information," Graham said. "Some individuals may not talk to me, because they don't know me and because they have that heartfelt past they don't want to share. They have painful memories of how they were treated during the era of segregation. Others will share that information, because they want the story to be told."

Graham also expressed her sadness at how a historic and beloved landmark has been neglected for so long.

"My ultimate goal is to put a book on the shelf and to put a marker on the entrance to the road to Paradise Park," Graham said. "My goal is to show that Paradise Park existed."

REMOVE RODMAN DAM

Robert L. Knight, Ph.D., Howard T. Odum Florida Springs Institute
(Reprinted from the Gainesville Sun, May 2013)

In my 1980 doctoral dissertation, I documented the plummeting decline in fish populations in Silver Springs and the Silver River compared to similar studies from the 1950s. My research was conducted about 10 years after the creation of the Rodman Pool and Dam on the Ocklawaha River and found that the formerly dominant fish, striped mullet and channel catfish, were no longer common in Silver Springs.

Other migratory species formerly known from Silver Springs, including striped bass and manatees, were also absent after the dam was closed. The Marine Mammal Commission and the Sea to Shore Alliance have recently stated that, with the phasing out of existing power plants with warm water discharges, the best hope for maintaining today's increasingly healthy manatee population in Florida is to facilitate access to springs, including "the removal of dams obstructing manatee access to major springs and river segments, particularly those along the Ocklawaha and Withlacoochee rivers."

Because these wildlife species were known to spend a good deal of their lives traveling the length of the St. Johns River and its tributaries, one credible hypothesis for their scarcity in Silver Springs was that the Rodman Dam was blocking their natural migration. Part of the ill-fated "Ditch of Dreams," the Rodman Dam has blocked the natural movement of fish and manatees between Silver Springs, the Ocklawaha River, the St. Johns River and ultimately the Atlantic Ocean since 1968. These single-minded animals, imprinted on the spring garden at the upstream end of the river ecosystem, are forever turned back by the insidious and purposeless invention of the defunct Cross Florida Barge Canal.

The entire St. Johns River ecosystem, consisting of its tributaries the Ocklawaha and Silver rivers, is in serious decline. Average annual flows in headwater springs are reduced by more than one-third. At least 20 springs formerly feeding the Ocklawaha River are flooded by the Rodman Pool and no longer flow. Base flows in the Ocklawaha and upper St. Johns rivers are reduced by one-half. Nitrate nitrogen concentration in the springs' once-pure water is now 24 times higher than it was before modern agricultural and urban development. This nitrate-laden groundwater is in part responsible for nutrient impairment all of the way downstream to the mouth of the St. Johns River.

Florida's state officials are waking up to a crisis that was in part created by promoting development regardless of the long-term environmental cost. Finally goaded by more than 25 years of water quality violations and highly visible explosions of noxious algae, our state and local governments are trying to decide who is going to pay to reduce nitrogen discharges to the surface and ground waters that support the St. Johns River ecosystem.

Our environmental agencies won't even admit that reduced spring and river flows are the result of excessive groundwater pumping. But in spite of that denial, many cities will soon need to turn to more expensive surface water supplies to solve the problem of lower aquifer levels and reduced spring and river flows.

In most cases restoration is expensive. Take the Everglades ecosystem where more than $20 billion has been spent to date. While some of the historic harm to the Everglades has been reversed by this expenditure, much more work remains to be done to restore the hydroperiod, water quality and wildlife populations that are dependent on a healthy Everglades. The cost for substantial restoration of the St. Johns River ecosystem will also be very high. These costs will ultimately be paid by Florida's citizens.

However, sometimes restoration can be relatively simple and even result in a savings for taxpayers. For example, annual maintenance of the existing Rodman Dam and Pool is estimated at $500,000. Over its 45-year life that is more than $20 million spent for a de-authorized project. Eventual rehabilitation of the earthen dam will cost even more.

In contrast, the cost of restoring the Ocklawaha River's natural flows, reopening the fish and manatee migration route to Silver Springs, and restoring the 20 drowned springs is estimated at $5 million. Partial removal of the Rodman Dam and the resulting benefits to the St. Johns-Ocklawaha-Silver River ecosystem may very well be the cheapest restoration project in Florida's history.

If the people of Florida really mean what they tell pollsters, and 80 percent of them believe that a healthy environment is critical to a healthy economy, then their voices need to be heard now. It is high time to restore the Ocklawaha River, its head waters at Silver Springs, and the entire interconnected St. Johns River ecosystem. Removing that dam structure would be a good way to start undoing the harm.

Unidentified steamboat on the Silver River c1872. Steamers regularly transported passengers between Picolata near Jacksonville on the St. Johns River via the Ocklawaha River to Silver Springs (Florida Archives).

DIVER EXPERIENCED SILVER SPRINGS
AS FEW HAVE DURING MAPPING EXPEDITIONS

Story by Marian Rizzo/ Correspondent
(Reprinted from the September 7, 2013, article in the Ocala Star-Banner Newspaper)

While most people are content to view the pristine waters of Silver Springs from a riverbank or while riding inside a glass-bottom boat, Eric Hutcheson wanted a closer look at the phenomenon beneath the surface.

So, in 1993, Hutcheson, a professional underwater cartographer, donned his scuba gear and dove into the world's largest artesian spring.

Among his tools were a plastic writing pad and a No. 2 pencil, plus a

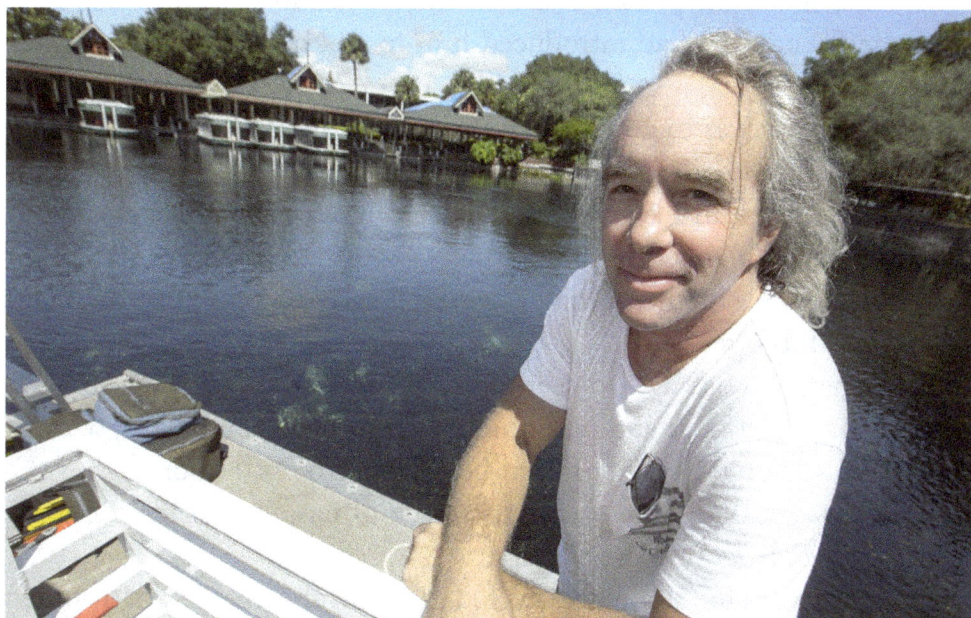

World renowned cave explorer, cartographer and artist Eric Hutcheson poses for a photo at Silver Springs on the Silver River on Wednesday September 4, 2013. This is the first time he has been back to the springs since ending his historic exploration of the cave system at the attraction in 1998. Hutcheson led a team that mapped as much of the system as could be explored.
(Alan Youngblood/OCALA STAR-BANNER)2013

roll of nylon string to measure distances and help him find his way out.

Funded by Florida Leisure Acquisition Corp., which owned Silver Springs at the time, the initial expedition consisted of six men, with Hutcheson as the head.

"They funded me to do exactly what I love to do," Hutcheson said. "They pulled out the red carpet so we could explore and map where nobody ever did before. All those underwater caves are like Mother Nature's artwork of the water sculpting through the limestone. There are layers and layers of Florida's sea bottom. It's a time capsule, and you are the first person to see it undisturbed."

The Silver Springs system consists of at least 16 springs, with the main one known as Mammoth Spring. Many of the cave openings are too narrow for most men, especially when loaded down with a bulky life support system. For Hutcheson, however, it was a piece of cake. During his early dives, he was 30 years old, 5 feet, 5 inches tall and weighed only 145 pounds. When confronted with a narrow opening, he simply removed his scuba tank and held it in front of him.

Hutcheson's hand-picked team included lead diver Ken Peakman, a longtime friend who had introduced him to sinkhole diving when they were teenagers.

"My specialty was to get through these really tight areas and continue exploring," Hutcheson said. "Ken would wait when I went beyond a certain area. There's an intimacy with who you're doing underwater exploring. It was like a safety blanket for me, mentally."

Others before Hutcheson had attempted early mappings of the main spring and didn't get far.

More than 50 years ago, former Silver Springs diver Jack McEarchern, with only a scuba tank and no lighting or mapping equipment, worked his way down about 20 feet to what he labeled "the fifth room." Now 83, McEarchern recalled with clarity the maze of passages inside the main spring. Some were only partially open.

"It didn't have a tunnel built so I could go in," McEarchern said. "I started moving rocks and dirt with my hands and went in as far as I could see. The sand would go off behind me, so I knew which way to go to get out. One time, I saw a piece of ivory tusk at the bottom of a little shaft the size of a 55-gallon barrel and seven feet down. I took my tank off and held it over my head. When I got down there and looked up and saw these rocks, I knew if one of them came loose it would have buried me right there, and I would have been one of them fossils. I never went back, not in that hole."

In an excerpt from Richard A. Martin's book *Eternal Spring*, longtime Silver Springs official photographer Bruce Mozert described the mystifying underwater scenes he encountered during his career.

"On cloudless days, when the sky overhead is a clear blue, the colors underwater take on a different quality—you might say a different color," Mozert wrote. "The blue of the sky is reflected in everything beneath the surface ... Similarly, on very bright, sunny days, a yellow-gold is predominant; and on dark, stormy days, incredibly deep greens and blues take the ascendancy."

Years later, when Hutcheson entered the main spring, he marveled at how the pure white limestone, with its bubbling fissures, instantly morphed to earth tones as the water flowed through porous rock inside the cave. On a cave bottom, Hutcheson's team discovered ancient fossils, wooly mammoth teeth and Indian artifacts. Though the exploration took his team through 2,263 feet of passages, they never reached the grand aquifer, and with good reason, Hutcheson said.

"I was trying to get there and we got really, really close," he said. "This is exploring way beyond the envelope. Silver Springs is a dangerous place because of the nature of the geology and the high volume of water eroding its passages. You could get down there in front of this volume of fresh, pristine water pushing you forcibly. It can't be stopped. There's a lot of pressure from the water that is boiling out of the springs. The ceilings are unstable. As you're moving through, the rocks move and block passages, and it becomes unsafe, which is why I stopped the exploration."

Even so, a lot of helpful data came out of Hutcheson's mapping of Silver Springs, said Scott Mitchell, director of the Silver River Museum, where some of Hutcheson's findings are on display.

"The value, I think, is that it helps us to understand the complexity of the Silver Springs cavern system and how it connects to the aquifer," Mitchell said. "What Eric confirmed was that it wasn't just a single hole in the ground, but an entire system and dozens of springs.

"The mineral formations are clues inside a cavern that tell whether it's gone through periods of wet and dry," Mitchell added. "Geologists and archaeologists can estimate how long it's actually been flowing and how humans have used the spring, whether they were living beside it or down inside it when it was dry. In caverns where the ceiling has come down, they've also been able to document how stable the cave system is. It was the culmination of 12 months of exploration. Eric dove repeatedly into the heart of the main spring, more than 90 feet deep and more than 300 feet from the spring's mouth."

Born in 1962 in Miami, Hutcheson attributes his mapping abilities to his grandfather, an architectural engineer who was involved in the early development of Miami.

As a youngster, Hutcheson was drawn to South Florida's tropical waters and flooded lime-rock pits where he played with his friends.

"We would swim and have a blast," Hutcheson recalled. "For my first experience with caves, I was 9 years old looking into the Biscayne aquifer. It was my first taste that those things exist."

In the late 1970s, Hutcheson's family moved to Ocala. That's when he met Ken Peakman, who introduced him to sinkhole diving. Whether they were dry or filled with water, the boys would work their way down to the water table.

"My mom would educate me, because we were just wild, young kids, and she would be worried," Hutcheson said. "She showed me some articles of people who were doing it right. I joined the National Speleological Society and was introduced to people who became my mentors."

Hutcheson's first professional project involved an exploration of Silver Glen Springs. Sanctioned by the Florida Department of Environmental Protection, the project was organized in 1989 by Bill Foote, owner of the Ocala Dive Center and a professional scuba diver. Foote selected Hutcheson as his lead diver.

"That launched my career. It was my first big break," Hutcheson said. "I used all the artistry of my grandfather's work, and then other opportunities, big cave projects, came immediately."

Since that initial dive, Hutcheson has been back to Silver Glen Springs multiple times. Over the last 25 years, Hutcheson has explored and mapped underwater caves in Florida, the Caribbean and in Mexico's Nohoch Nah Chich, the world's longest underwater cave system with more than 50 miles of passages. He assisted with lighting and other underwater projects for National Geographic magazine, contributed a chapter in "Aquiferious," a book about Florida's springs by artist Margaret Ross Tolbert, and his art and cartography have been featured on the Discovery Channel, Animal Planet and the Learning Channel. Hutcheson's work can be viewed at www.visionfromthecaves.com.

Tragically, Hutcheson's underwater ventures came to a halt following a motorcycle accident in 2000. He suffered multiple injuries, including a severely damaged sinus cavity. Since scuba diving was no longer an option, Hutcheson became involved in his family's business producing plaster architectural molds for high-end homes.

Then, in 2005, while on vacation with his wife, Sharon, and daughter, Erika, he went snorkeling in a tank at Discovery Cove in Orlando. When he reached 15 feet underwater, his sinuses popped.

"That was the first time that I could actually clear my ears and equalize the air pressure, which would allow me to dive again," Hutcheson said. "This huge part of my life has come full circle and I'm out doing it again."

For Hutcheson, one of the driving forces behind his work has been the

World renowned cave explorer, cartographer and artist Eric Hutcheson, right, enters the cavern with Dr. Joe Wallace in the main spring at Silver Springs on the Silver River on Wednesday September 4, 2013. This is the first time he has been back to the springs since ending his historic exploration of the cave system at the attraction in 1998. Hutcheson led a team that mapped as much of the system as could be explored. (Alan Youngblood/OCALA STAR-BANNER)2013

preservation of the Floridan Aquifer.

"Silver Springs has taken a huge blow," Hutcheson said. "It's lost more than half of its volume in the decade that was a huge development period. We're swimming in rainfall that fell 200 years ago. Today, it's been compromised. Silver Springs is not fed from one source. It's fed by sources from all over the place. The nitrate levels are high."

Now that Hutcheson is diving again, he would like to do more exploring at Silver Springs. One of his concerns is that less-experienced divers also will want to try cave diving there.

"Exploring underwater caves to the limit is probably one of the most dangerous things a person can do," Hutcheson said. "There's a lot of death in this kind of thing. I've lost dozens of colleagues and probably a handful of close friends."

According to Foote, while snorkeling is permitted in the county's three springs areas, scuba diving is not. Foote is part of a group of scuba diving enthusiasts that includes local businessmen and members of law

World renowned cave explorer, cartographer and artist Eric Hutcheson checks algae growth in the eel grass on a steam boat wreck at Silver Springs on the Silver River on Wednesday September 4, 2013. This is the first time he has been back to the springs since ending his historic exploration of the cave system at the attraction in 1998. Hutcheson led a team that mapped as much of the system as could be explored. (Alan Youngblood/OCALA STAR-BANNER) 2013

enforcement. He said they have outlined a plan to gain state approval to bring scuba diving back to Silver Springs, but there have to be some safety parameters.

"We're proposing, for the first year, especially, not having any open water students diving there," Foote said. "Divers will have to be certified. They can't be learning how to dive."

YOUR WATER, YOUR MONEY, SILVER SPRINGS, AND THE PUBLIC TRUST

Robert L. Knight, Ph.D., Howard T. Odum Florida Springs Institute
(Reprinted from the Gainesville Sun September 2014)

Your state government is hard at work—spending hundreds of thousands of your tax dollars to fight environmental advocates trying to protect Silver Springs, the Silver River, and the Ocklawaha River from further degradation.

During five days last week, the petitioners: Karen Ahlers and Jeri Baldwin, the Sierra Club, the St. Johns Riverkeeper, and the Florida Defenders of the Environment, joined forces in a David and Goliath struggle against Canadian billionaire Frank Stronach's Sleepy Creek Lands (a.k.a. Adena Springs Ranch) cattle operation near Fort. McCoy. Against all logic, the St. Johns River Water Management District was on the wrong side of this legal contest.

At stake was the transfer of an existing 1.46 million gallons per day (MGD) groundwater permit from a former sod farm to the first phase of Stronach's grass-fed beef operation. After two-and-a-half years of negotiations that reduced the requested groundwater use from an average of 13.2 to about 5.3 MGD for about 17,000 cows on nearly 30,000 acres, the applicant and District decided to divide the ranch project into multiple phases. In May the District recommended issuance of water quality and groundwater pumping permits for the first phase.

Over 4,000 acres of timberland have already been cleared to accommodate more than 6,000 cattle. Instead of relying on Florida's abundant rainfall to water their grass, Sleepy Creek plans to use over 200 gallons of aquifer (i.e., spring) water per cow per day to increase their profit margin. But this extra profit comes at a staggering cost to the public.

The petitioner's experts made the following demonstrations of fact. First, the previous permittee, Johnson Sod Farm, was actually using about 0.2

MGD and not the permitted 1.46 MGD, and therefore the transferred permit actually allows an average 1.26 MGD increase in groundwater use, inflicting further harm at Silver Springs and the Ocklawaha River.

The 6,400 cattle planned for Phase 1 will produce an estimated 158 million pounds of manure and 11,000,000 gallons of urine per year. The irrigated grass will require about 700,000 pounds of nitrogen in fertilizer, in addition to the cow wastes. These cumulative nitrogen loads are expected to contribute additional pollution of the region's surface and groundwaters.

While the District's consultant opined that 1.46 MGD is a "small" groundwater extraction, in fact, it would authorize the cattle operation to divert a total of 10.7 billion gallons of water that would otherwise nourish the area's springs over the 20-year permit period.

Another way to look at 1.46 MGD is to realize that at current average Florida per capita water use rates, this permitted quantity could provide a perpetual water supply for about 10,700 people.

While the District has recently determined that the aquifer feeding Silver Springs is over-allocated by more than 30 MGD, and the whole District is facing a serious shortage of water for public supply, District management is so eager to appease this applicant that they expended hundreds of thousands of taxpayer dollars to defend the issuance of this permit. This money was spent on at least four District lawyers, a dozen or more District staff professionals, and at least four outside consultants billing up to $250 per hour for hundreds of hours each.

Earlier this year the District committed to spending $20 million on springs' projects that they claim will eliminate more than 700,000 pounds of nitrogen pollution per year and reduce existing groundwater withdrawals by up to 1.5 MGD. Those problems are just the tip of the iceberg of springs impairments caused by previously permitted projects. The obvious irony is that a simple denial of the Sleepy Creek permit would have accomplished the same goals and saved the taxpayers $20 million.

A public hearing was held as part of the permit challenge. With only two days of notification, about 100 people showed up at District headquarters in Palatka to plead with the judge for permit denial. The public's testimonies were taken under oath and entered into the official record. Their words were both inspiring and heart-breaking.

Sleepy Creek's neighbors are already suffering intolerable consequences, including the sight of wild animals driven from their forest homes by land-clearing, swarms of biting flies, failure of adjacent private wells, and discharges of manure-filled surface runoff into wetlands. Dozens of concerned citizens described the former beauty of Silver Springs and their dismay over its current sad condition due to declining flow and increasing nutrient pollution.

The petitioners, those individuals and environmental groups who are trying to protect Florida's springs and rivers, had to raise more than $150,000 in donations to fight this Phase 1 project. Still, there is no guarantee of success and it will be months until the state's hearing officer makes a final ruling. In the meantime, the sheer injustice of the District issuing a permit to a private corporation in the face of falling aquifer levels, impaired springs and rivers, and over the objections of thousands of local citizens is unfathomable.

Florida's water law is clear. Every permitted groundwater extraction needs to be in the "public interest." The public has bravely spoken that the proposed Sleepy Creek water use is not in their interest. The District should listen more closely to the people whose environmental treasures they are entrusted to protect. It is not too late for the District's Governing Board to right this mistake and to boldly deny every new and existing permit that further harms the public trust.

Original Art by Rob Smith.

GETTING THE WORD OUT TO 'SEE SILVER SPRINGS'

Story by Marian Rizzo/ Correspondent
(Reprinted from the September 13, 2013, article in the Ocala Star-Banner Newspaper)

Allen O. Skaggs joined the staff at Silver Springs in 1962. After Bill Ray resigned to start his own public relations firm, the Ray family contacted Skaggs, who was working in public relations at the University of Florida at the time. Nancy Werhner stepped back in time recently, when she began sifting through the belongings of her mother, Lucile Skaggs Stewart, who died suddenly in January. In Stewart's treasure trove were numerous reminiscences of her first husband, Allen O. Skaggs, who was public relations director at Silver Springs in the 1960s.

Allen Skaggs Jr., left, was head of public relations for Silver Springs from 1962-69. He was honoree of the chiefs and given the name "Achamee" by the Seminole indians in the '60s. He is pictured next to Will Rogers Jr., center, and Jo Dan Osceola, right, chief of the Seminole Indians at the time. (Doug Engle/Ocala Star-Banner) 2013 (Florida Archives)

Among the memorabilia, Werhner found mastodon teeth, brochures touting Florida facts, fliers promoting Silver Springs, a 45 rpm record with songs about Silver Springs and Weeki Wachee, an embroidered Seminole Indian jacket, photos of movie stars who had toured the park and a pile of newspaper clippings about her father.

"I lived at the springs in the summertime," Werhner said, as she looked through her treasures. "We swam there. My mom would drop me off and I would ride the boats. And, for a couple of months one summer, I sold pearls in one of the kiosks. After church on Sundays, Silver Springs was a very popular area. You could hardly get in the front gate. We'd go in the back way and up to my father's office. It overlooked the entire park."

Skaggs joined the staff at Silver Springs in 1962. After Bill Ray resigned to start his own public relations firm, the Ray family contacted Skaggs, who was working in public relations at the University of Florida at the time.

"It was a big risk," Werhner said. "My mother often said if my father had known they were going to sell to ABC, he probably never would have left UF. Things changed a lot after ABC's takeover. They brought in their own people. It wasn't a family-oriented business anymore. It had lost the closeness."

When Skaggs arrived at Silver Springs, an aggressive publicity campaign had already been started by the Rays and co-owner W.M. "Shorty" Davidson. Hundreds of billboards lined the highways in the southeastern United States, and numerous promotional films, TV ads, bumper stickers, fliers and road maps went nationwide with the message, "See Silver Springs."

Having worked in public relations at UF, Skaggs easily adapted to the fast-paced campaign at Silver Springs.

"He was a workaholic," Werhner said. "He worked seven days a week, 12 hours a day. He loved to cook, so when he came home, usually after 7 or so at night, he would cook out on the grill and relax. Aside from going to the beach every summer, my father would hardly ever take a vacation. He was relentless in his pursuit of promoting Silver Springs in the state of Florida, both as an educational tool and as a place of natural beauty. He just loved Silver Springs."

Being a teenager at the time, Werhner was enthralled by the famous people her father lured to the park. Besides politicians and businessmen, he arranged tours for such stars as Burt Reynolds, Morey Amsterdam and

Darby Hinton, a child actor who starred in the *Daniel Boone* TV series. If Skaggs heard that a famous person, like Dan Blocker (Hoss in *Bonanza*), was at Six Gun Territory, he would invite him to visit Silver Springs.

"Buddy Ebsen was one of my father's fraternity brothers at the University of Florida," Werhner said. "He came to tour Silver Springs."

Werhner also recalled eating lunch at the same table with Rock Hudson and Claudia Cardinale, who were filming *Blindfold* at Silver Springs.

"I was pretty star-struck," Werhner said. "They both were such huge movie stars."

                                      ~

But, for Skaggs, the glitter was just a small part of what he did. Long-time Silver Springs employee Leon Cheatom said Skaggs also mingled with the park staff.

"His main objective was to get the people there, but once we got 'em there it was up to us to satisfy them with the boat rides and the shows," Cheatom said. "He was a hands-on type of fella. If you got busy, he'd help out. He would pitch right in. If the lines at the glass-bottom boats were long, he would come in and help line up the people. And, out front, where they were selling tickets, he would even go in the ticket booth itself and open up another window to help take care of the people."

While she was attending college, Arrilla Jones Milby worked part-time as Skagg's secretary. In a phone interview from her home in south Daytona, Milby said sometimes Skaggs would send her out of the office to do some underwater modeling for the park's photographer, Bruce Mozert.

"Whenever I went to work, I didn't know if I was going to be in the office or in the water," Milby said. "It was the best job I've ever had. I left to get married or I probably would have stayed there a lot longer. Mostly, I typed letters for Mr. Skaggs, business letters or 'thank you for coming' letters. We had a lot of scrapbooks and I would work on them also. I was told that all of them had been thrown away, and I said, 'Please, don't tell me that, because that's the history of the springs.'"

During ABC's ownership, Mozert and Skaggs also made a film called *Mr. Outdoors.*

"I shot it, and Allen wrote the story," Mozert said. "It was about an old man who lived in the forest. He knew all about wild animals and underground springs. A lot of it was shot at Silver Springs, underwater and down the river. I'd say two-thirds of it was about Silver Springs."

~

Born on March 6, 1916, in Urbana, Ill., Skaggs attended Gainesville High School, then majored in English and journalism at the University of Florida. Later, he returned to teach both subjects there. Werhner noted that she and her sister Sharon Thierer, of Fort Myers, followed in their father's footsteps.

"I was an English teacher for 38 years in Ocala. I retired from Vanguard in 2010," Werhner said. "My sister was public relations director of Tiki Gardens in St. Petersburg and then went on to work for several politicians. She was Sen. Connie Mack's aide in his Fort Myers office when she retired."

After graduation, Skaggs worked for several Florida newspapers, including the *Plant City Courier*, the *Suwannee County Democrat* in Live Oak, the Florida State News in Tallahassee and *The Gainesville Sun*, where he held jobs as city editor and sports editor.

Skaggs joined the staff at UF in 1942, became the university's news bureau chief and was president of the Florida Public Relations Association. As a member of the administrative council, he promoted an "open door" policy with the press. He also was chairman of the University Lecture Series and acted as an escort for many visiting politicians, including John F. Kennedy and Richard M. Nixon, before they became president. Skaggs also served on the board of the First United Methodist Church in Gainesville. And, he helped create a brochure for the First United Methodist Church of Ocala. Skaggs worked at UF for 20 years until he was invited to be public relations director at Silver Springs. In a quote in the school's alumnus newspaper, Skaggs conveyed his excitement about his new job.

"This will be a tremendous opportunity and a challenge to continue my dedication to the state of Florida and its greatest resource—tourism," Skaggs said. "This job has a breadth of public relations opportunities rarely found anywhere."

Dr. Steve Gilman, an Ocala orthopedic surgeon, was a medical student at UF when Skaggs worked in public relations there. He recalled that Skaggs seemed very knowledgeable in that area.

"When he finally left Gainesville and came to Silver Springs, it was back in the days when Silver Springs was a big attraction," Gilman said. "Allen was very good at his job. He put out fliers all over the country."

While living in Ocala, Skaggs served as president of the Florida Tourism Council and the Florida Attractions Association. He spearheaded a highway program to install orange colored markers that gave the mileage to Florida's major tourist attractions, including Silver Springs.

～

The American Broadcasting Company bought Silver Springs in 1962. Skaggs stayed at the park until 1969, then left to form his own public relations business. Less than two months later, he died of a heart attack at the age of 53, on March 23, 1969, while attending a travel conference at Cypress Gardens. His obituary was in multiple newspapers throughout the state. His wife Lucile saved them all.

Nancy Werhner reacts when remembering what she had to eat at Ross Allen's house when she was younger. "I hated going over there for dinner. Ross liked to make fried grub worms, rattle snake and bear," Werhner said in disgust. Werhner's dad, Allen Skaggs Jr., was head of public relations for Silver Springs from 1962-69. He was also President of Florida Attraction Assoc. and Pres. of Florida Tourism Council. He passed away in 1969 when Nancy was a Senior at Ocala High School. "He died of a heart attack at Cypress Gardens," Nancy said Friday afternoon, September 6, 2013 at her mother's home. She was surrounded by tons of memorabilia from the park and pictures of movie stars from that era including Rock Hudson and Burt Reynolds. (Doug Engle/Ocala Star-Banner) 2013.

Thinking back on her father's career, Werhner said some of his best days were at Silver Springs. She recalled his close relationship with Buck Ray Sr. Besides working together, they organized groups from the staff to go hunting and fishing.

Jack McEarchern remembered the fun they had on some of those outings. Like the time McEarchern, Skaggs and Florida Cracker tales author Dave M. Newell decided to tie a live turkey to a tree so Buck Ray would believe he actually killed some wild game.

"Buck had this ol' double-barrel hammer gun," McEarchern recalled. "We heard that ol' hammer come back and he shot and killed that turkey. Allen was the one who got the turkey, but everybody in the camp knew what was goin' on. Buck picked that turkey up and under the wing was a sign that said, 'See Silver Springs.'"

A TIME OF RECKONING

Robert L. Knight, Ph.D., Howard T. Odum Florida Springs Institute
(Reprinted from the Gainesville Sun, February 2015)

The health of North Florida's springs may soon become the principal consideration that determines our region's economic future. The 1,000-plus natural artesian springs arranged along the Santa Fe, Ichetucknee, Suwannee, North and South Withlacoochee, St. Johns, St. Marks, and other spring-fed rivers, are collectively informing us that there is a breaking point beyond which society should not venture.

A growing realization of excessive environmental harm is putting the brakes on the runaway over-exploitation of finite natural resources. Sustainable use of the groundwater in the Floridan Aquifer and the finite assimilative capacity of the aquifer for nitrogen contamination have been exceeded. Diminished springs filled with greening water and noxious algae are symbolic of these inconvenient truths.

Tallahassee politicians are singing the virtues of North Florida's springs and allocating increasing tax dollars to springs restoration projects. Having eliminated the Florida Springs Initiative during his first year in office, Governor Rick Scott now appears to be concerned about springs. In 2011, Governor Scott was handed a facemask and snorkel by springs artist and author Margaret Tolbert and received an invitation to visit area springs. The Governor left the snorkel and mask untouched on the floor below his chair when the event was over.

Recently while surrounded by admiring environmental advocates, Governor Scott pledged to spend $1.6 billion dollars on springs restoration and protection over the next 20 years, and $50 million in this year's budget. These are amazing promises. But two of the questions we all must ask are: "why did our state government allow such a disaster to happen in the first place?" and "will our money be spent wisely?"

First, "why did our government allow special interests to exceed the natural limits of the Floridan Aquifer in terms of water withdrawals and nitrogen contamination?" The simple answer is because of economic gain for the elite few. It certainly was not in the public's best interests to over-allocate this limited groundwater resource or to apply excess nutrients that wound up in our drinking water supply.

Second, "can we rely on this same state government to spend our tax dollars wisely?" The short answer is no. It is unsettling to imagine that an excessive share of the tax dollars currently earmarked in the name of springs protection could wind up in the pockets of private, for-profit, corporations who contributed most to these problems in the first place.

Approximately $70 million was allocated by state and local sponsors in 2014 for engineering fixes to impaired springs.

Based on the state's own calculations, the estimated average cost per million gallons per day (MGD) of groundwater saved by these projects will be about $1.7 million. The Florida Springs Institute has estimated that a reduction of about 1,400 MGD of groundwater pumping will be necessary to protect Florida's springs. It follows that restoring spring flows through engineered projects is likely to cost in the billions of dollars.

The average cost to reduce nitrogen loads to the Floridan Aquifer based on the state's 2014 springs protection grants was estimated as $178 per pound of nitrogen. Considering that nitrogen in fertilizer only costs between $1 and $7 per pound, this is a hefty price for taxpayers to shoulder to protect polluters.

Prevention is always cheaper than restoration. Groundwater use could be greatly reduced by collecting an Aquifer Protection Fee (APF) for all uses. City dwellers in Florida currently pay from $3 to $10 per 1,000 gallons. A fee of as little as $1 per 1,000 gallons for all users, including agriculture and self-supply wells, would discourage wasteful and inefficient water uses, while generating about $875 million each year. For comparison, bottled water currently costs about $1 per gallon ($1,000 per 1,000 gallons). APF funds could be used to subsidize water conservation measures, develop surface water supplies, finance springshed protection, and pay for aquifer and springs monitoring.

Likewise, an APF of about $1 per pound of nitrogen should be placed on all nitrogen-containing fertilizers in the Springs Region of North and

Central Florida. This proposed APF would raise an estimated $154 million each year. The resulting increase in fertilizer cost would also result in more efficient agricultural practices, which, combined with restrictions on landscape fertilizer use, would result in a reduced load of nitrate-nitrogen to the aquifer and springs.

Putting the entire burden of springs restoration and protection on the backs of taxpayers who do not directly profit from free water and low-cost fertilizer is poor state policy. Legislative creation of an APF puts the greatest costs on those who use the most groundwater and nitrogen fertilizer—typically those corporations and individuals who currently profit the most at the public's expense.

Former swimming platform and glass bottom boats in Silver Springs c1950
(Photo by Bruce Mozert, Florida Archives).

LONGTIME JOURNALIST TELLS THE SILVER SPRINGS STORY

Story by Marian Rizzo/ Correspondent
(Reprinted from the September 26, 2013, article in the Ocala Star-Banner Newspaper)

While many different people were making history at Silver Springs Attraction over the years, one person was busy memorializing their efforts.

David Cook, a *Star-Banner* journalist and local historian, has been documenting and writing about Silver Springs off-and-on since 1953. Though such stories are but a drop in a bucket compared to Cook's stockpile of other historic happenings in Marion County, Silver Springs made a lasting impression on him in both his professional work and his personal life.

Born July 29, 1927, in Delray Beach, Cook moved with his family to Ocala when he was 4 years old. Though Cook was very young at the time, he recalled hearing adults talk about how Silver Springs operators Carl Ray and W.M. "Shorty" Davidson were feuding with M.R. Porter over his plans to develop a park on the south side of the Silver River and call it Silver Springs Paradise.

"My dad was angry at the way Ray and Davidson were treating Mr. Porter," Cook said. "My dad sided with Mr. Porter. He was just enraged with Ray trying to put Mr. Porter out of business. Of course, Mr. Porter was trying to put them out of business too. He played by the rules, but Ray used every means he could get."

Eventually, Paradise Park changed hands, first to a Jacksonville business group, and, ultimately, to Ray and Davidson, who, after exhausting lawsuits, finally broke down and purchased it, Cook said.

After that, development continued to increase on both sides of the river.

By the time Cook was 8, Silver Springs had become a favorite recreation spot, particularly on Sundays.

"We'd have afternoon picnics on the grounds," said Cook. "We went to the free beach a little ways down the run. Children could wade in there.

The bathhouse fee was a quarter, but most of us kids just wore our swim-suits and just went right in swimming. They had thatched huts where the adults spread out the picnic lunch. We didn't ride the boats because it cost too much money."

Cook recalled that his Boy Scout troop also congregated at the park. Silver Springs herpetologist Ross Allen hosted Boy Scout jamborees there, he said.

"We caught water snakes at Orange Lake and sold them to him. He fed them to his reptiles," Cook said. "Orange Lake was just alive with them. We waded out in the swamp up to our waist. I think we got about 12 bucks for a bag of snakes. At that time, that was a lot of money. You could get into the movies for a quarter."

Cook was about 12 when MGM studios brought Johnny Weiss-muller to Silver Springs to film *Tarzan Finds a Son*. A classmate of Cook's, Gooley Green, doubled for Johnny Sheffield, who played Boy.

Cook said the stars wanted nothing to do with the critters, so Green doubled for scenes that showed him hitching a ride on a turtle or being chased by an alligator.

"A lot of us kids went out to Silver Springs to catch a glimpse of Johnny Weissmuller. Of

David Cook looks through some of the many pictures of the Silver Springs he has collected over the years in the Star-Banner office in Ocala, FL on Tuesday September 17, 2013. Cook was a reporter and editor at the Ocala Star-Banner covering the area for more than 40 years. (Alan Youngblood/OCALA STAR-BANNER) 2013

course, we were all greatly impressed," Cook said. "Ross Allen and Newt Perry did some of the animal wrestling scenes. And one of Newt's sisters was a stand-in for Maureen O'Sullivan (Jane)."

For a brief period, Silver Springs sported a diving tower on the beach. It had a 10-foot-high diving board and a 20-foot diving platform. For Cook, who was a teenager at the time, the temptation was too strong.

"I jumped off it one time and scraped my nose on the bottom," he said. "The water was only about 10 feet deep. When you're diving, you go straight down. Somebody must have dared me, or probably some girl was watching and I had to show off."

While in high school, Cook worked as a soda jerk at a local drug store. He also started contributing articles to the *Evening Star* before it merged with the *Morning Banner* to form the *Star-Banner*.

During his junior year, Cook served as a page for the House of Representatives in Washington, D.C. Even then, he was busy documenting his experiences.

"I kept a diary and a notebook of all the famous people," he said. "One of my clients was Clare Boothe Luce. And, I remember having lunch at the White House with Eleanor Roosevelt and meeting the president. I left Washington primarily to come home and graduate with my class."

Cook said he spent a lot of time at Silver Springs in his early days. Getting there was easy. He either rode his bicycle or hitchhiked on Ocklawaha Avenue (now Silver Springs Boulevard). During World War II, buses started running to Silver Springs. The fare was only 25 cents, Cook said.

"We continued to swim there throughout World War II years and into the early '50s," said Cook. "When I got married, my wife and I went to the free beach. Then they closed it because of insurance costs. They'd had some accidents between the boats and swimmers at the head springs. They stopped swimming at the head springs too."

Cook enlisted in the Army Air Corps in 1945 and served for 18 months, mostly in Iceland. He was released when the war ended.

Cook believes Silver Springs's heyday began after the war ended and the nation started pulling out of the Great Depression.

"During World War II, people couldn't buy a car or gas," said Cook. "After the war, people started traveling again. And, what did people do? They hit the roads and Silver Springs flourished."

Under Ray and Davidson, several attractions already had been established at the park. Ross Allen founded his reptile institute. Colonel Tooey began to operate the jungle cruise boat ride. And, movie companies started coming to Silver Springs, beginning with the *Tarzan* film series.

The owners also made improvements on the glass-bottom boats. By 1950, more than 800,000 visitors a year were coming to Silver Springs, park data states. Meanwhile, Cook used his GI bill to complete four years of college in three at the University of Georgia, earning a degree in journalism. His first daily newspaper job was at the *Moultrie (Ga.) Observer*.

In 1953, Cook moved back to Ocala and worked as a sports editor and general reporter at the *Ocala Star-Banner*. In time, he moved up to city editor, and eventually became editor-in-chief.

Cook left Ocala in 1967 to take a job as assistant editor of the *Tallahassee Democrat*, then, 12 years later, he returned to the Star-Banner as managing editor. He also wrote a political column and a historical column.

When he retired in 1995, he continued his historical column, naming it "The Way it Was."

Cook had only been with the *Star-Banner* two years when he got a frantic call from Bill "Blue" Ray, one of the owners of Silver Springs.

"He called me at around 6 o'clock in the morning and said, 'Grab your camera and get out here. Silver Springs is burning,'" Cook said.

According to the park's records, the estimated damage to ticket booths, shops, the cafe and other structures was $250,000.

Former Silver Springs photographer Bruce Mozert said Cook was a familiar face at the park, over the years.

"He was always good to us. He was there for, good Lord, years and years. He wrote several stories on me at different times over a period of years."

Now that control of Silver Springs is reverting to the state, Cook expressed some concerns.

"I'm always leery when politicians have their finger in anything," he said. "They find a way to get their fingers on the money. Things get done that aren't in the public interest. But I prefer the state having it than the local government. If the County Commission controlled the springs, they'd have contractors approaching them with some scheme to make money on it. In my opinion, it shouldn't be about making money, but about public convenience."

In addition to his work at the *Star-Banner*, Cook was a former chairman of the Marion County Historical Commission and was a former member of the Marion County Historical Society and the Florida Historical Society. He also wrote the book, *Historic Ocala, The Story of Ocala &Marion County*, which was commissioned by the Historic Ocala Preservation Society in 2007. Cook and Mariam, his wife of 60 years, have four daughters, seven grandchildren and two great-grandchildren. At 86, Cook continues to write his weekly column, "The Way it Was."

"It's an important legacy," said Buddy Martin, an author and WOCA radio personality on "The Voice of Ocala."

"I go back to the early days with David Cook," Martin said. "I worked at the *Star-Banner* in the 1960s. I was sports editor when I was in my early 20s, and he was city editor. But the David Cook I know best is the one who writes the history of Ocala, and I am grateful for it. I think the next generations are reconnecting with the past, and David has helped them make that transition."

David Cook looks through some of the many pictures of the Silver Springs he has collected over the years in the Star-Banner office in Ocala, FL on Tuesday September 17, 2013. Cook was a reporter and editor at the Ocala Star-Banner covering the area for more than 40 years. (Alan Youngblood/ OCALA STAR-BANNER) 2013

THE PEOPLE'S PLAN

Robert L. Knight, Ph.D., Howard T. Odum Florida Springs Institute
(Reprinted from the Gainesville Sun, August 2015)

Staff at the Florida Springs Institute (FSI) have been active in the scientific study of Silver Springs since the 1970s. FSI's efforts, as well as research conducted by the State of Florida have demonstrated severe biological impairments at Silver Springs as a result of reduced flows, elevated nitrate nitrogen concentrations, and lost connectivity to the St. Johns River. All of these detrimental impacts are a result of human actions, are reversible, and are contrary to Florida laws that protect the biological integrity of Outstanding Florida Waters such as Silver Springs.

For more than four decades, the State of Florida has had laws that were intended to protect the flows, water quality, and natural functioning at Silver Springs. For most of that 40-year period state agencies have been finding reasons to delay the removal of the Rodman Dam on the Ocklawaha River. In 2001, fourteen years ago, state water managers started to develop a rule to limit further flow reductions at Silver Springs. Two years ago, the Florida Department of Environmental Protection finally initiated a plan to limit increasing nitrate pollution at Silver Springs.

To-date, none of these long overdue efforts is complete, while additional permits for groundwater pumping and pollution are still being issued. Even more embarrassing for the state's environmental agencies is that the draft versions of these restoration efforts such as DEP's recently released draft Basin Management Action Plan, even if fully implemented, will fall far short of restoring the health of Silver Springs.

To help fill this interminable gap, FSI prepared a comprehensive restoration plan for the Silver Springs System in 2014. FSI's Silver Springs Restoration Action Plan describes a feasible approach to restore the historic flow at Silver Springs, reconnect the Silver and St. Johns rivers, and lower nitrate-nitrogen concentrations to protective concentrations. This

"People's Plan" represents the public's best interests rather than the special interests that have influenced the state's insufficient restoration efforts thus far. Comprehensive restoration of Silver Springs will be dependent upon returning the system as closely as possible to its historical physical, chemical, and biological conditions. Existing restoration planning efforts by state and local governments have not slowed Silver Springs continued decline.

FSI's Silver Springs "People's Plan" outlines a specific set of actions that will improve the natural condition of the river in the short-term (next five years) and will ultimately (next 20 years) restore it to a near-pristine historical condition. During the first five years of this proposed restoration effort, it is critical that the state legislature mandate collection of Aquifer Protection Fees" on all groundwater and nitrogen uses to encourage voluntary efficiency and conservation efforts.

FSI's recommended water quantity restoration goal for Silver Springs is to increase existing average spring flows to >90% of their historic average of 520 million gallons per day (MGD). The average flow of the Silver River over a recent decade (2003-2012) was 345 MGD (more than 33 percent below historic flows). This flow recovery goal will require a groundwater pumping reduction of about 132 MGD in the regional area that affects flows at Silver Springs. This goal can be accomplished through the state's existing permitting procedures if they are properly enforced.

FSI's and the state's initial target for nitrate-nitrogen concentration reduction at Silver Springs is a maximum monthly average of <0.35 mg/L, which equates to a 79 percent reduction in nitrogen loads to the vulnerable portions of the springshed. A substantial portion of this nutrient reduction can be accomplished in concert with the water quantity restoration described above. Cutting back on permitted groundwater extractions for agricultural and urban irrigation will have the beneficial side-effect of reducing nitrogen fertilizer use. Human wastewater nitrogen loads in the springshed can be reduced by implementing advanced nitrogen removal for all central wastewater plants and by providing centralized collection and wastewater treatment for all high-density septic tank areas.

Removing the Kirkpatrick Dam on the Ocklawaha River is a priority to provide open passage for aquatic wildlife between the Atlantic Ocean, the St. Johns River, and Silver Springs. Breaching the dam will increase the diversity and dominance of fish and other aquatic wildlife species within the river ecosystem. These native aquatic vertebrates have been shown to optimize the photosynthetic efficiency of the Silver Springs System, increasing the forage base that supported the formerly diverse and abundant fish and wildlife populations that utilized Silver Springs.

Reduced spring flows, increasing concentrations of nitrate-nitrogen, and a downstream dam impeding the movement of aquatic fauna

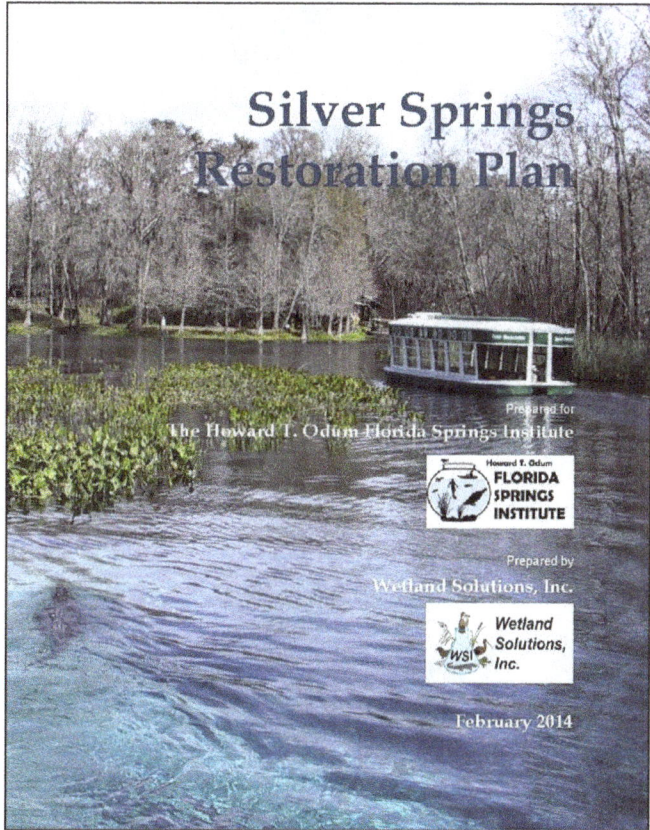

are resulting in visible long-term changes to the natural flora and fauna of Silver Springs. While the past cannot be changed, the future can be. This springs' restoration opportunity should not be lost as a result of weak enforcement of existing laws by politically-motivated state and local governmental agencies. Ecological restoration of Silver Springs will require a holistic approach for dealing with all sources of impairment simultaneously, rather than a piecemeal approach of delayed and divided responsibilities. It is time to fully implement the "People's Plan" for a restored Silver Springs.

FORMER MODEL RECALLS DAYS FILMING UNDERWATER

Story by Marian Rizzo/ Correspondent
(Reprinted from the November 7, 2013, article in the Ocala Star-Banner Newspaper)

Ginger (Stanley) Hallowell strolls through her 1950s vintage home and points out her collection of mermaids, treasured Weeki Wachee lamp and posters of her passed out in the arms of a scaly monster from beneath the sea. She pauses over a pile of scrapbooks that bulge with newspaper clippings depicting her longtime career in modeling—above

Ginger Stanley Hallowell, former underwater model at Silver Springs, is shown at her Orlando, FL home on Friday September 20, 2013. Hallowell was the stand-in for the underwater scenes in the Creature from the Black Lagoon and can be seen in photos with Ricou Browning. The Ray family sent her to the Gary Moore Show in New York to promote the park, and she did numerous other promotional photos and engagements, working primarily with Bruce Mozert. (Alan Youngblood/ OCALA STAR-BANNER)2013

122

and below the water. Included are numerous photos taken by Bruce Mozert at Silver Springs, where, from 1953 to 1956, she worked under public relations director Bill Ray. Now 81, Hallowell remembers those days with clarity.

"Bill Ray was just a couple of years older than me," she said. "He was always thinking of fun things to do. He would get with Bruce and say, 'What could we do to send to the newspapers?' I spent half my time with these great, huge scrapbooks pasting in all these clippings from every newspaper in the country and some out of the country. Everything we did was picked up by the Associated Press or some other news service."

Hallowell was caught on film talking to fish, shooting an arrow at a target, grilling hot dogs and clipping eel grass, plus going to picnics, circuses and dinner parties—all underwater.

Among Mozert's favorites was a sequence of photos done with a TV set and a lounge chair.

"We had a big ol' television underwater. It looked like it had a screen on the front, but it was just flimsy paper," he said, stifling a laugh. "Ginger was supposed to be a mermaid, and Ricou Browning was sitting there looking at her. She comes out and sits on his lap. Then the wife comes with a frying pan and hits him over the head."

Always striving for something better, Mozert dreamed up different breathing techniques to help his models stay underwater longer. His team planted hoses in accessible locations and ran them up to a compressor on the surface. But, he said, there were challenges.

"We got this idea to put a paint compressor up above and hook two hoses to it, one for Ginger and one to my helmet," he said. "We were down 40 feet. I would take a breath and she wasn't getting anything. Then I'd stop and she'd take a breath. As soon as she took a swig, water would come up in my helmet, so I'd hold my breath until the water came down. I'd exhale to push the water down and I'd drink the rest of it. We learned we couldn't breathe at the same time. Somebody was going to get drowned. What we did, we put a valve on it for her."

Mermaid in the Movies

Hallowell swam as a double for Julie Adams in *Creature from the Black Lagoon*, filmed in 3-D at Wakulla Springs, and doubled for Lori Nelson in

Revenge of the Creature, filmed at Silver Springs, with underwater scenes shot at Marineland near St. Augustine. Hallowell did not perform in *The Creature Walks Among Us*, the third film of the trilogy.

One of the most memorable scenes was an underwater ballet sequence featuring Hallowell and Ricou Browning, swimming double for the creature. While she was swimming near the surface, he moved beneath her using matching strokes.

"We just dreamed it up," she said. "Water would go into Ricou's eyeholes, so the only way he could see me was to turn upside down. During the whole sequence, he was supposed to be swimming underneath me and I wasn't supposed to know he was there. Every now and then I'd feel this scaly hand come up and skim my leg or my bottom and I'd say, 'Oh, Ricou must be there.'"

In a phone interview from his home near Fort Lauderdale, Browning said he met Hallowell at Weeki Wachee Springs, where he was an underwater show producer and she was a mermaid. It was there they learned underwater hose breathing techniques.

When Browning took a job as assistant public relations director at Silver Springs, Hallowell was already working there. He recalled the day Hallowell, then 23, set a record for swimming the 7-mile Silver River.

She wore a rubber wet suit, face mask and fins, and she used an aqua lung, which she had to swap out four times during her 3½-hour swim.

"I supported her in doing that," Browning recalled. "I was in and out of the water to look out for her. She was a gutsy little gal. She was a good swimmer, and she did whatever was asked of her."

Hallowell worked as an extra in such films as *Distant Drums*, *Splash II* and *Passenger 57*, and doubled for Esther Williams in *Jupiter's Darling*, shot at Silver Springs and Weeki Wachee. Because of a perforated eardrum, Williams was unable to do deep-water swimming, Hallowell said.

"They could only do close-ups of her face," she said. "They put me in to do the swimming. So it was her face and my swimming."

When off the set, visitors would stop Hallowell, thinking they had found Williams.

"I signed autographs in her place," Hallowell said. "I signed my name, of course. They had me made up in the same costume and matching auburn wigs to look as much like she looked as possible."

From the spring to the stage

Born Dec. 19, 1931, in Georgia, Hallowell, with her parents' permission, moved to Sebring when she was 15 to live with her older sister, Chris Grant. Hallowell met Newt Perry while she was competing in a watermelon festival in Leesburg. She was sponsored by the Ocala Jaycees, and Perry had brought a mermaid from Weeki Wachee to the competition.

"He said he was looking for swimmers who don't look like swimmers," Hallowell said. "He asked if I'd be interested in trying out as one of the mermaids. I couldn't believe they were staying underwater for four or five minutes, but I agreed to train. Anytime someone said to me, 'Would you do this or that?,' I would say, 'Yes,' and it always turned into something good."

Hallowell worked at Weeki Wachee for 2½ years. After her sister moved to Ocala, Hallowell visited her on weekends and sunbathed at Silver Springs. One Saturday, Bruce Mozert saw her swimming and decided to test her as an underwater model. They had to be able to hold their breath for at least two minutes. Hallowell did, and she ended up working for Mozert on weekends. In 1953, she left Weeki Wachee and came to work at Silver Springs full-time. While in Ocala, Hallowell performed with the Marion Players and was the bad girl in the play *John Loves Mary*.

"I did that at night and would swim during the day," she said. "I would go with wet hair to rehearsals, straight from Silver Springs to the stage."

The small screen

Hallowell's promotional work also took her to New York City for a CBS talent exhibition on the *Gary Moore Show*.

"They set up a tank on the stage. I got in and sat and ate an apple, drank a bottle of juice and wrote my name on a slate," Hallowell said. "They mostly wanted to show I could sit underwater and do all those things. A hose was attached to a scuba tank. I had to swallow before I could take another breath or I could choke. We were taught to do that at Weeki Wachee."

Barbara Walters was working behind the scenes arranging talent for shows, Hallowell said. Walters called her back just before Thanksgiving to be an underwater weather girl for guest host Dick Van Dyke.

"Barbara Walters dreamed up a big tank with a map on the side," Hallowell said. "I used a white cosmetic stick to put in snow and rain for three time zones. On Thanksgiving Day, I ate a turkey leg underwater while doing the weather."

Hallowell's promotional tours included a porpoise Christmas show at Marineland and an underwater performance on the *Alec Gibson Show* in Miami Beach.

Though sometimes paid by different venues, she promoted Silver Springs wherever she went.

Preserving the memories

In 1956, Ginger Stanley left Silver Springs, married Albert V. Hallowell Jr. and moved to Orlando, where she got a job at Channel 6, the only TV station in town at the time. She hosted a 15-minute women's talk show called *Browsing with Ginger,* and left when she was expecting her first child.

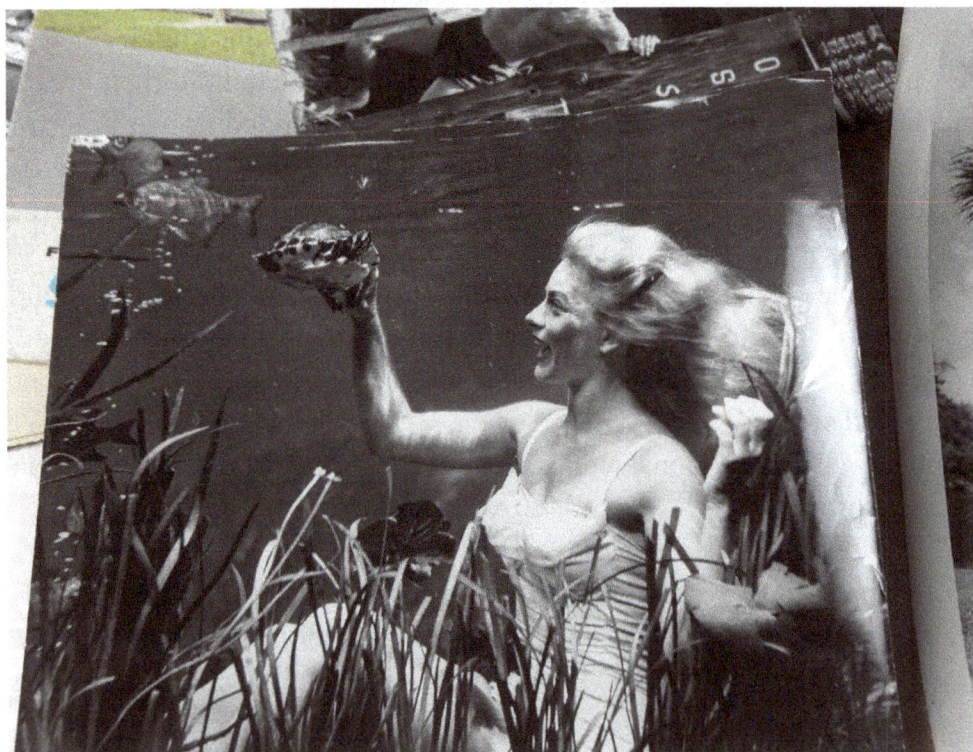

Ginger Stanley Hallowell, former underwater model at Silver Springs, was in all kinds of pictures for advertising and promotions as well as underwater. Hallowell was the stand-in for the underwater scenes in the Creature from the Black Lagoon and can be seen in photos with Ricou Browning. The Ray family sent her to the Gary Moore Show in New York to promote the park, and she did numerous other promotional photos and engagements, working primarily with Bruce Mozert. (Alan Youngblood/OCALA STAR-BANNER)2013

Afterward, she spent 23 years as a runway model for charities and department stores, and for Walt Disney World. She also posed for a brochure promoting the Marion Oaks subdivision.

Hallowell has been featured in multiple magazines and on 11 covers, from *Skindiver* to *Scary Monsters Magazine*. In 2002 and 2003, she and Browning were celebrity guests for Creaturefests in Tallahassee. In 2012, she was inducted into the Mermaid Hall of Fame while celebrating the 65th mermaid reunion at Weeki Wachee.

Albert Hallowell died of heart disease in 1987. Ginger retired 11 years ago. She has three daughters and six grandchildren. She stays active line dancing and teaching exercise classes at a senior citizen facility.

Opening the photo albums revived the wild and wonderful memories of her past.

"I want all of it preserved," she said, a sparkle in her eyes.

"I miss the fun of the underwater more than I miss the fashion shows," she added. "To dream up all this stuff and do something unique was fun. Where else could you do that? It didn't pay much money, probably $60 a week at Silver Springs, but it was plenty for me to live on. What I did was what other people considered hard work, but I thought it was fun."

GLASS HALF FULL?

Robert L. Knight, Ph.D., Howard T. Odum Florida Springs Institute
(Reprinted from the Gainesville Sun, April 2016)

The fate of Florida's groundwater resources rests on the accuracy of mathematical models. Scientists and engineers estimate groundwater flows and levels by collecting and summarizing data from wells, rivers, and springs, and then use computers to simultaneously solve thousands of equations to give the best fit between actual and modeled groundwater levels and spring and river flows. Problems arise when the model's conceptual aquifer structure does not match reality and when computer-generated model parameters are not constrained by real aquifer characteristics. The result is that groundwater flow models often include significant discrepancies between actual and predicted groundwater levels and flows.

The Florida Springs Institute (FSI) enlists highly qualified technical advisors to provide independent review of the models that are used by the state to manage groundwater resources. Those experts have concerns about the poor quality of the models used for evaluation, review, and issuance of water-use permits by the Water Management Districts (WMDs) throughout Florida. Based on information provided by the WMDs, it is apparent that many of the existing groundwater flow models have not been thoroughly reviewed, validated, or used with adequate caution. Without proper review, water managers and the public cannot have confidence in the results provided by these models.

Complex groundwater-flow models need to be thoroughly reviewed by competent professionals with no vested interest in the outcome of the reviews. Scientific peer review comments need to be addressed with appropriate model modifications. The FSI recommends that each model be reviewed by at least two independent peer reviewers, followed by full public disclosure of review comments, and documentation of how the models are revised to effectively incorporate suggested improvements.

The limitations on the application of the models should also be thoroughly addressed. It is imperative that the accuracy of every groundwater-flow model used for allocating groundwater pumping permits be estimated and reported along with model predictions.

For example, many of the models prepared for water-use permitting are intended for regional analysis and yet they are applied to site-specific permitting applications. Gross overestimates of groundwater availability appear to be the norm. Model estimates of spring flow reductions due to groundwater extractions are strikingly different from actual measured changes in spring flows.

The St. Johns River WMD's best models estimate that Silver Springs flow has been reduced by about 5 percent by groundwater pumping while actual average flow reductions are greater than 30 percent. The Southwest Florida WMD's groundwater model estimated that pumping had lowered flows at the Gum Slough Springs Group by 3 percent while actual data show a 50 percent spring flow decline. And the Suwannee River WMD groundwater flow model predicts an average decline in Ichetucknee River flows of 5-9 percent while an independent analysis by the U.S. Geological Survey documented a 23 percent decrease.

The degree to which groundwater modeling errors impact efforts to protect springs was most clearly revealed two years ago after independent experts reviewed the model used by the St. Johns River WMD to establish minimum flows and levels for Silver Springs. The WMD model initially indicated that pumping had such a negligible effect on Silver Spring's flow that additional groundwater withdrawal permits could be issued before significant spring impacts occurred. After the outside review, the WMD admitted that flows at Silver Springs were already more than 12 million gallons per day past the point of significant harm. Efforts by the WMD to address that impact are still underway. The salient point is that the state's model was drastically wrong, and if not for independent review, the error might not have been caught.

A more recent groundwater modeling effort was initiated by the state in 2014 to better assess the cross-boundary effects of massive groundwater withdrawals in northeast Florida and southeast Georgia. This model, named the North Florida Southeast Georgia (NFSEG) model includes the same flawed framework as the previous WMD groundwater flow models. These models all include the simplifying assumption that the Floridan Aquifer does not include caves and large underground conduits, a conceptual error that leads to unreasonable aquifer characteristics contradicted by actual data. It is not reasonable to expect a measurable improvement in the accuracy of groundwater pumping impact estimates provided by this new and "improved" NFSEG model.

On behalf of all citizens in Florida who wish to have a sustainable groundwater future, FSI advocates for a full and truly independent review of the NFSEG model before it is adopted for issuing the next round of groundwater permits. The public cannot tolerate another inaccurate and unbelievable conclusion that additional groundwater withdrawals will have no impact on our dying springs and lakes.

Silver Springs is famous for its lovely models. However, a different kind of model—a seriously flawed, mathematical groundwater flow model—is being used by state officials to justify excessive water extractions from the Floridan Aquifer, ultimately threatening the health of the aquatic wonderland that was Silver Springs.
Bruce Mozert photographing Ginger Stanley underwater at Silver Springs in 1955.
From the Bruce Mozert Collection, Florida State Archives).

MODELS RECALL STUNTS, CAMARADERIE OF SILVER SPRINGS

Story by Marian Rizzo/ Correspondent
(Reprinted from the November 13, 2013, article in the Ocala Star-Banner Newspaper)

A group of Silver Springs models from the 1950s and '60s recently crammed into Bruce Mozert's tiny photo studio for a reunion that included hugs, memories and funny stories. The women, now in their 70s and 80s, shared the moment with Mozert and also Jack McEarchern, a veteran Silver Springs employee who appeared in several magazine ads with the ladies.

As the park's longtime photographer, Mozert lived what many men might consider "a dream job." He got to work with a bevy of lovely young

Four of the former Silver Springs mermaids, Betty Frazee Haskins, left, Ginger Stanley Hallowell, Arrilla Jones Milby and Pat McLauchlin Nelson all pose for Bruce Mozert next to pictures of themselves from the '50s Wednesday. "I could hold my breat for 3-4 minutes. I didn't ever smoke," local photographer Bruce Mozert said Wednesday afternoon, September 1, 2010 at the Piccadilly restaurant. "This is the first time we've had all the girls, except Mary Thomas together." Four of the former Silver Springs mermaids gathered for lunch and remembered the good ol' times when they worked at Silver Springs. Mozert, who is the father of underwater photography, photographed the girls above and below the water to publicize the park. (Doug Engle/Star-Banner)2010

girls who worked in the public relations office under Bill Blue Ray but were available at Mozert's beck-and-call for modeling assignments.

But Mozert had a strictly professional attitude. Recalling the parade of beauties that came through the park, he said he simply viewed them as photographic art.

"It was no different than shooting a two-by-four," Mozert said. "They were just human beings to me."

Arrilla Jones Milby, of south Daytona, said she felt comfortable posing for Mozert, who always treated them with respect.

"He was the A-one photographer as far as I'm concerned," Milby said. "He never used bad language around me. He was a very strong, moral man, and I appreciated that so much. I've been in touch with Bruce over the years. Every time I come through Ocala I stop and say hi to him. He's a Christian and I'm a Christian. The last time I was there, I was able to sit down with Bruce and share what Jesus has done for us."

Modeling for Mozert had its creative moments, particularly during the holidays, Milby recalled.

"For the Fourth of July, I had a rocket strapped to my back and I was lighting the fuse. But, it was just a prop," she said.

There were occasional scary incidents, like the time she was posed with a live bear.

"I was supposed to have some chocolate in my mouth, and he would come up and take it out," she said. "His tongue went from my chin to my forehead taking that candy out of my mouth. When I ran out of candy, he pushed me to the ground."

In Mozert's studio, Milby reminisced over photos of herself and her friends, Pat McLauchlin Nelson and Betty Frazee Haskins. Some were simple, everyday poses with the girls doing household chores or playing sports. At other times, they shared the lens with some of Silver Springs' wildlife.

"We were either very brave or we were very young and dumb," Haskins said. "I once wrestled an alligator for a movie, and Ross Allen had to come out and show me how to do it. The ideas came from Bruce and Bill and Ricou Browning—he was a real idea man. I think they sat around all day thinking of something for us to do."

In his early 20s, John Ming worked for Mozert at the park, shooting photos of people on the glass-bottom boats and taking pictures of some of the models.

"A lot of the crazy stuff happened before I came there," Ming said. "I left for a while to help my father with his commercial fishing business. When I came back to the springs, my primary job was to take cheesecake pictures of the girls in different kinds of funny settings. If you got an idea, you made it work. That's basically what Bruce was doing. He had a terrific imagination. When the girls came to work in the morning, they didn't know what they'd be doing. Bruce would get an idea, and the next thing you know, they're standing there in a bathing suit or short-shorts and away we went. We put their faces up all over the country. That was a job I would have worked at for free while the Rays had it."

It was Haskins who invited Nelson, now of Gainesville, to the park. Nelson also attended Reddick High School, where she was a cheerleader and Haskins was a drum majorette. After being hired at Silver Springs, the two did several promotional projects together.

"It was a fun job," Nelson said. "Here I was, a little country girl, going to New York and getting to go on *The Today Show* with Dave Garroway. They did a thing on Florida bathing beauties and three of us went from Silver Springs."

Though most of her shots were considered cheesecake, Nelson recalled some hair-raising stunts, like the time she had to stand near a large diamondback rattlesnake Ross Allen brought to the set.

"I'm terrified of snakes," Nelson said. "They froze it with a fire extinguisher. Then, they set up all these metal reflectors to put the light where they wanted it. The reflection off the metal kept thawing out the snake. I was ready to climb the nearest tree. They had to keep freezing it and then thawing it out."

While working at Silver Springs, Nelson became a judge for the Miss University of Florida contest when it was held at the park. Actress Faye Dunaway, then a student at UF, was runner-up.

Nelson was crowned Miss Sebring Grand Prix in 1958. She also posed for a *Seventeen* magazine swimsuit article shot at Silver Springs and did underwater stunts for a couple of *Sea Hunt* episodes.

Those were the days before Photoshop and other photographic enhancements, so the girls' natural beauty had to come through. But Mozert had some tricks of his own, Nelson said. For one, he had the girls stand on their toes so their muscles would tense up for a streamlined look.

"Bruce always said, 'Suck in your gut and wet your lips,'" she said. "None of us were very tall, so he would always get down and shoot up on us."

For Luresa Lake, posing for Mozert was an opportunity of a lifetime. She still has the Paradise Park brochure she modeled for in the late 1940s. On the cover, Lake is leaning against the trunk of a palm tree with the text, "Sunbathing is fun at Paradise Park on Silver River near Ocala, Florida."

"That picture went on the wire and the brochure went all over the southeast," Lake said.

Lake was working in a county office that attended to the needs of Ocala's black residents when Paradise Park manager Eddie Leroy Vereen asked her to pose for promotional photos.

"I was quite pleased, because, in the first place, I became a model. That, by itself, was great to me, because there weren't that many black models in the state," Lake said. "Mr. Vereen was looking for young black ladies that were attractive in Ocala. I was available because I lived in the city of Ocala and was convenient to Silver Springs."

Now 83 and active with Shady Grove Missionary Baptist Church, Lake came to meet with the other models at Mozert's studio.

"The peculiar thing about life, after you get old, you don't travel or get around as much as you used to," she said. "It's the most wonderful thing, every now and then, if you might see some of those people who were in the pictures."

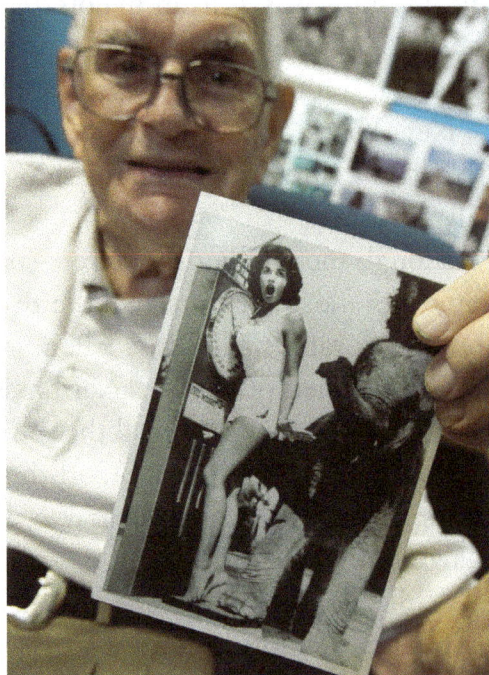

Photographer Bruce Mozert shows off one of his comical pictures that he took of model Pat McLauchlin with a baby elephant stepping on the scales, while he was a photographer at Silver Springs Attractions in the 1950s. He and five of the former models met at his studio Monday afternoon, September 23, 2013. The girls use to model for Silver Springs and the Ray family, who owned the park, back in the '50s. (Doug Engle/ Ocala Star-Banner)2013.

IT'S RAINING, IT'S POURING

Robert L. Knight, Ph.D., Howard T. Odum Florida Springs Institute
(Reprinted from the Gainesville Sun, June 2017)

Florida is the fifth rainiest state in the U.S., receiving an annual average of about 150 billion gallons of rain per day (BGD). In the approximately 1,400 square miles that feed groundwater to Silver Springs, average rainfall supplies about 3.4 BGD. On average, only about 15 percent of this rain finds its way into the Floridan Aquifer.

In the first half of June, the Silver Springshed received an estimated 200 billion gallons of rain. This rain resulted in a jump in spring flows, and rising well levels throughout Alachua, Lake, Marion, Putnam, and Sumter, the four counties that feed groundwater to Silver Springs and water supply wells. The welcome rain soaked the parched earth, revitalizing pastures,

Glass bottom boats at Silver Springs in the 1950s (Photo by Bruce Mozert, Florida Archives).

lawns, crops, forests, and wetlands. And this rain breathed additional life into our region's mighty springs, gasping from declining flows over the past 50 years.

Despite Nature's bounty from the sky, North Florida continues its reliance on groundwater for irrigation of urban lawns and agricultural crops. Average flows at Silver Springs have progressively declined by more than 36 percent, from a pre-1970 average of about 520 million gallons per day (MGD), to an average of 330 MGD during the past decade. An estimated 120 MGD of the measured flow reduction at Silver Springs is due to the net consumption of groundwater extracted through wells.

Studies conducted throughout Florida's Springs Region indicate that any reduction in flow is harmful to a spring's environmental health. Reduced flows result in lower aquatic plant production, decreased wildlife populations, and less ability for a spring to cleanse itself of noxious algae and pollutants.

While no flow reduction would be preferable for maintaining healthy springs, some groundwater is needed for agricultural and urban development. Due to an inter-dependence on groundwater resources, natural environments, especially springs, suffer as the human economy prospers. If an acceptable balance between competing aquifer uses is not achieved, then the combined health of humans and the environment suffers as well.

Florida's water laws anticipated this conflict in 1972 with passage of the Florida Water Resources Protection Act. This law required the state's five water management districts (WMDs) to adopt minimum flows for springs that would protect them from harm caused by competition for finite water supplies.

This year the St. Johns River WMD finally adopted a minimum flow rule for Silver Springs. The WMD's rule claims to protect 94 percent of the natural flow at Silver Springs. But this goal is difficult to assess since the District bases compliance on a complex and imprecise groundwater flow model. This assessment should be improved by incorporating the actual measured flows at Silver Springs into the analysis.

After accounting for rainfall declines, existing average flows at Silver Springs are down more than 120 million gallons per day, a decline of more than 20 percent of historic levels. The ecological effects of these excessive flow reductions are clearly visible—more noxious algae, declining water clarity, and diminished fish populations. The data tell us that groundwater pumping in and around the Silver Springshed needs to be reduced by more than 90 million gallons per day to comply with the WMD's minimum flow target.

Despite this deficit in natural flows, the WMD continues to issue new groundwater pumping permits. Spring flow reductions have been recorded throughout North Florida, with a 20 percent decline at Rainbow, more than 50 percent decline at Crystal River, and up to 40 percent or more throughout the more than 200 springs in the Santa Fe and Suwannee River drainages.

The old proverb, "when it rains, it pours," has more than one meaning. On one hand, it sums up recent weather in North Florida. Mother Nature has been more than generous in her liquid bounty. Hopefully, everyone has turned off their sprinklers.

But on the other hand, this phrase reminds us that misfortunes often follow each other in rapid succession. The same type of model used by the St. Johns River WMD is being used to manage minimum flows at these other springs. In fact, these new rules authorize increased groundwater pumping, and additional harm to the region's springs.

The defenseless springs are not being guarded by state officials. Please raise your voice and speak for the springs.

MODEL RECALLS HEYDAY AT SILVER SPRINGS

Story by Marian Rizzo/ Correspondent
(Reprinted from the December 19, 2013, article in the Ocala Star-Banner Newspaper)

Betty (Frazee) Haskins has been on the cover of magazines and has won several beauty pageants, but the limelight she cherishes most was when she modeled for photographer Bruce Mozert at Silver Springs in the late 1950s.

Haskins, a golden-haired country girl from Reddick, fit the hometown look Mozert was looking for in models. He posed them doing everyday activities in such settings as kitchens, picnics and playgrounds, often setting the stage underwater at the bottom of the main spring. Haskins, one of the most photographed of Mozert's models, said it was obvious he wanted to portray the park's wholesome atmosphere in his photos.

"This was what they tried to put across, that Silver Springs was a family place, with lots to do outdoors," Haskins said. "Bill Ray was a stickler for it. He said it was a very family-oriented park and we were like a family there. That's why they called it the Silver Springs family."

Born in Jacksonville, Haskins moved with her family to Ocala when she was 10 years old. She attended Reddick High School before it merged with other rural schools to form North Marion High School. Haskins, a drum majorette, was performing with the school band at Silver Springs when public relations director Bill Ray offered her a summer job in his office.

Ocala photographer John Ming was Mozert's assistant when Haskins first came there.

"Bill Ray was always on the lookout for models," Ming said. "Betty came in and we did a photo shoot to see if she was photogenic, and she was very photogenic."

After graduating from high school, Haskins accepted an invitation to work fulltime at Silver Springs. Much to her mother's dismay, this ended her plans for college.

"The principal told my mother he could get me a scholarship," Haskins said. "But I had a different kind of education. It was a lot more fun. Clippings came in every day for their scrapbook at Silver Springs. Dozens would come in of the same picture so I kept a personal scrapbook."

Haskins still has a pile of magazines, and her scrapbooks are filled with photos showing her in a variety of poses, such as reclining on a large clam shell or grilling a steak underwater.

Those underwater shots came with some effort, she said, while crediting her accomplishment to Ricou Browning, a former underwater show producer for Weeki Wachee Springs and the swim double for the *Creature from the Black Lagoon.*

Betty (Frazee) Haskins was one of the top two models who did most of the photography work with Bruce Mozert at Silver Springs. Betty also did some promotional traveling for the Springs. She shows off some of her memorabilia at her home in Laurel Run Wednesday afternoon, September 25, 2013. "I had 20 magazine covers and competed in the 1958 Miss Florida. I was second runner up, but I got first in face and figure, if anybody cares," Haskins said with a chuckle. (Doug Engle/Ocala Star-Banner) 2013.

"Ricou was my mentor and my instructor in scuba and how-to-do tricks underwater, like drinking a Coke and eating a banana," Haskins said. "We worked on breath control and learned how to pose underwater without making a mess or stirring up the sand."

TV and Movie Time

Though she came to be known as one of Silver Springs "mermaids," the only time Haskins donned a tail was for her underwater role in the Jerry Lewis film *Don't Give Up the Ship*, filmed at Silver Springs. Haskins said she and Florence McNabb, a former Weeki Wachee mermaid, worked for three days on a part that got only five minutes of film time.

"It was in the winter and the water was cold," Haskins said. "We wore wool knee socks underneath the tail. It was a satin-like material with sequins on it and it was very heavy."

Because they were underwater for long periods of filming, the two mermaids had to use air hoses.

"We each had an airman," Haskins said. "My personal savior was Ricou Browning. I would signal for air with my hand at my throat and Ricou would swim in with an air hose. The airmen had to let us breathe and then swim completely out of the picture. This was at the bottom of the spring, 50 feet deep. They had placed artificial kelp on the floor to make it look like the bottom of the ocean. One time, Ricou got his fin tangled up in that and was slower getting back than I wanted him to be."

Haskins said when the swimmers were at such a depth for so long they had to be careful not to surface too quickly.

"It could be dangerous," she said. "You could get the bends. But Ricou and Bill Ray were experts. They definitely trained us how to use all the gear and how to be safe with it. They taught us how to do deep breathing before getting in the water. It expands your lungs and puts oxygen through your system so you're able to hold your breath longer. They did a good job of making us feel safe."

For her movie role, Haskins joined the Screen Actors Guild and got union pay, $100 a day, while her salary at Silver Springs was $50 or $60 for a six-day week.

Haskins' other movie credit was *Women of Wongo*, a Tropical Pictures film in which she wrestled a six-foot alligator.

She swam in an underwater sequence for the *Arlene Francis* TV show and did some underwater swimming in four episodes of the *Sea Hunt* TV series. In one episode she rode on the back of an 800-pound sea turtle, 40 feet below the surface. In another, which was titled *The Girl in the Trunk,* Haskins was placed in a straitjacket and was locked inside a trunk at the bottom of the main spring.

"I took one last gasp from a hose and they closed it and put chains around it," she said. "That was a scary one. I was counting—one, two, three, four. I began to think, I hope I live through this. Then a diver comes in and gets the chains off, and Ricou comes in with an air hose—and the director says, 'Cut.'"

Mega Model

It wasn't long before Haskins got her good friend Pat McLauchlin Nelson into the act. A cheerleader at Reddick High, McLauchlin joined the Silver Springs team and went with Haskins to New York City, where they appeared on Dave Garroway's *Today Show* and Steve Allen's *Tonight Show.* They also made an appearance at boat shows in New York and Boston, on behalf of boat companies, all the while promoting Silver Springs.

Haskins' modeling career also took off. She was in numerous articles and on the cover of about 20 magazines, including the *Boston Globe's Sunday Magazine* and four covers of *Skin Diver.* She posed for Mercury Motors and several boat company advertisements, which were shot at Silver Springs, Lake Weir, Mill Dam and the Ocala Boat Basin, and she did a photo shoot in exercise attire for *McCall's* magazine. Ocala photographer Jim Jernigan photographed her for a 1987 issue of *Sequoia Communications.*

One of Haskins' favorite photos was one Mozert shot at Silver Springs. The staff took a large block of Styrofoam and carved it to look like an iceberg. It had a Mercury Motors engine on the side and Haskins on top with a pair of ski poles.

"Everything they did was so clever," she said.

For a promotional ad for the March of Dimes, she was photographed wearing a bathing suit with 1,000 dimes attached. She rode the Jai Alai float in the Gasparilla Parade in Tampa, accompanied Browning to the Jacksonville Naval Air Station to demonstrate scuba equipment to a boys' club and did a week of promotional shots for the Sarasota Chamber of Commerce.

Haskins entered several beauty pageants, taking the crowns of Miss Lake Weir, Miss Sebring Grand Prix and Miss Florida Public Relations. She was runner-up in the Miss Citrus Queen and Miss Florida contests. Even more special, park staff named her Miss Silver Springs for three consecutive years.

"It wasn't a contest, but it was the most important one to me because it started me on everything else that I did," Haskins said.

Haskins left Silver Springs to marry professional baseball player Hayden Haskins in 1960. He died of a heart attack in 1993. Now 73, Haskins has two children and one grandson.

In 2011, she attended a *Sea Hunt* reunion that included a Sea Hunt Club.

"They called themselves Sea Hunters. I would compare them to the Trekkies," Haskins said. "They thought I was a big star and wanted my autograph. I was thrilled."

MANY HANDS MAKE LIGHT WORK

Robert L. Knight, Ph.D., Howard T. Odum Florida Springs Institute
(Reprinted from the Gainesville Sun, July 2017)

I am frequently asked if I think Florida's springs will be saved. My standard answer is simple, "Only when enough people understand and care about springs (and the rest of Florida's environmental woes) to affect true political change."

Perhaps you are already aware of the army of individuals who have dedicated themselves to achieving this challenging goal. We write newspaper op-eds. We teach civic-minded advocates about the challenges and solutions. We conduct the science documenting the declining springs' health and devise techniques for springs' restoration. We give dozens of lectures and interviews each year around the state to political leaders, state agencies, non-governmental groups, reporters, churches, and schools.

But, despite additional taxpayer money being spent, more empty promises coming out of Tallahassee, and numerous attempts to clean up our waterways through the ever-confusing alphabet soup of regulation (*i.e.*, FDEP, TMDLs, BMAPs, BMPs, MFLs, etc.), Florida's springs' health continues to decline.

Luckily, with a worthy goal in sight, there is always a way to overcome obstacles in the path. In the case of our springs, the worthy goal we are all striving for is a sustainable and prosperous human economy, living in harmony with a restored and protected Florida environment. That goal can be attained by reducing excessive reliance on free groundwater for almost all our water uses, taxing pollutants such as nitrogen fertilizers at the source to reduce their use and visioning a future Florida where quality of life is more important than quantity.

These ambitions will not be achieved without the combined will and support of the voting residents of Florida, and a new state government that is responsive to the public's long-term best interests. I believe these changes will only be made through education and eventual adoption of a new water ethic that instills enhanced civic pride in all citizens.

The question before us now is, "How many Florida voters must be educated and ultimately stand together to change the anti-environmental political system currently in power?"

Google tells us that there are about 9 million voters in Florida, and that about 50 percent, or 4.5 million, turn out for a statewide election. If we assume that there are enough candidates who will represent the public welfare over corporate profits, we will need about 2.3 million voters to elect a majority of legislators who might reverse the fate of dying springs. Can that many Floridians join their hands for a common cause?

In 2015, the Florida Springs Council was formed for this specific purpose. The Florida Springs Council is a private, non-profit 501(c)(3) tax-exempt organization. Any group or association can join the Florida Springs Council by committing to share their common goals to, "Ensure the restoration, preservation and protection for future generations of Florida's springs and the Floridan aquifer that sustains those springs and provides our drinking water." In less than two years, over 45 environmentally focused organizations have joined the Florida Springs Council, and those

Copyright 1905 by the Rotograph Co.
G 15687 "Gigging for big Fish," Silver Springs, Fla

Gigging for big fish at Silver Springs c1905 (Florida Archives).

organizations already represent more than 350,000 individual members in Florida. This is what might be called a good start!

To advance the goals of aquifer and springs protection, the Florida Springs Council provides technical input to the State of Florida on water use permit decisions, regional water supply plans, Minimum Flows and Levels and Recovery Plans, and Basin Management Action Plans. When state environmental agencies adopt plans that are not protective of springs, the Florida Springs Council supports both legal and non-legal challenges to improve those plans. The Florida Springs Council also works to develop and promote legislation that prevents further degradation or pollution of Florida's water resources. And, the Florida Springs Council continually endeavors to educate the public about our precious springs and the actions needed to restore and preserve them for future generations.

For individuals who feel powerless to affect social and environmental change, the Florida Springs Council is a beacon of light in the darkness. Many hands uniting in support of a common cause can and will make lasting changes for the better.

PARK MANAGER HONORED FOR WORK AT SILVER SPRINGS

Story by Marian Rizzo/ Correspondent
(Reprinted from the March 28, 2014, article in the Ocala Star-Banner Newspaper)

Sally Lieb leaned against a rail fence at Silver Springs State Park, the waters of the main spring rippling behind her, and broke into a wide grin as she talked about the joys and challenges of recreating Marion County's prized landmark. Though she stands a mere 5 feet 2 inches tall, as park manager Lieb has big plans for renovating the historic 4,460-acre venue.

"I'm all about nature," Lieb said. "This is such an opportunity to bring Silver Springs back to a world-class status as a state park. It's nice to be in on the groundwork of that."

Park Manager Sally Lieb is shown at the main spring at Silver Springs State Park in Silver Springs, FL on Thursday March 27, 2014. The park is undergoing a restoration to a more natural state since the State of Florida Department of Environmental Protection took over the former tourist attraction in October.(Alan Youngblood/Ocala Star-Banner) 2014

From the time she took on this project, Lieb said she has thought of little else. "I'd wake up at 2 o'clock in the morning thinking about a list of all the things I had to do," she said. "I wanted a lot of things for people to do to get them away from technology. We're starved for the natural world."

There is no question Lieb is comfortable in her element. She was born in Carrolltown, Pa., and graduated from college in 1979 with a bachelor's degree in biology. She soon began working in jobs that dealt with the care of animals and natural resources.

Lieb joined the Florida Park Service in 1993 and served at several state parks, including Homosassa Springs, Manatee Springs and the Payne's Prairie Preserve, before coming to Ocala in 2011 to manage Silver River State Park.

When the Silver Springs Nature Park reverted back to state control, Lieb became park manager of both areas, which were combined to form Silver Springs State Park.

Every transition comes with its own challenges, Lieb said.

"You kind of have to look at each spring on a case-by-case basis and identify what the impact is before making decisions on what you can do to help," she said.

Currently operating with a staff of 16 and a growing volunteer base, Lieb wants to return the park to its natural setting. That means getting rid of invasive exotic plants such as skunk vine and cat's claw, as well as paper mulberry trees that have overgrown the area previously used for the Jeep Safari ride.

To that end, Lieb uses non-polluting herbicides. Other ecological measures include using pine bark mulch instead of cypress shavings. Cypress trees are needed in the wetland, she said.

Scott Mitchell, director of the Silver River Museum, has already observed Lieb's intense commitment.

"For a lot of the changes to the infrastructure, the decisions are made in Tallahassee, and then Sally receives a mandate to make them happen, often with limited resources," Mitchell said. "She's done a very good job of managing this transition of a private attraction to a state park, which has been a massive undertaking."

Mitchell said the citizen support organization, the Friends of Silver Springs State Park, also has grown under Lieb's management. Since her arrival, he said, several trails have better signage, making them more accessible to visitors. And, Mitchell noted, Lieb also formed a volunteer river patrol.

"It's not as ominous as it sounds," Mitchell said. "They maintain a presence on the river and offer to help people that might need some assistance if they're broken down. Or, if they're getting too close to feeding the monkeys, they give them a friendly reminder that it's dangerous. They also interact with visitors on the river and answer questions."

Mitchell said Lieb's certification as a burn boss has filled another need at the park.

"She has already jumpstarted a prescribed burn program," he said. "You will see her with a fire suit on and she'll be in the thick of it with the rest of them, digging trenches and prescribing burns. Before we had Sally, we had to bring in a burn boss from another park."

Mitchell said the Silver River Museum also has benefited by Lieb's presence.

"She provides a great deal of support to the museum," he said. "For example, when we had Ocali Country Days, her staff jumped right in and helped us. To sum it all up, Sally's been the right person at the right time for Silver Springs."

Honored for her work

Early this year, Lieb, 57, was named the 2013 Employee of the Year for District 3 of the Florida Park Service. On March 4, during a volunteer appreciation dinner, she was honored as the 2013 Employee of the Year for all five districts in the system. Donald Forgione, director of the DEP's Florida Park Service, made the presentation.

In an email message, Forgione wrote: "I am very proud of Sally Lieb and the work she has done leading staff and volunteers to bring Silver Springs into the family of award-winning state parks. It's been a big job and she has worked through many challenges."

Lieb was initially nominated by her supervisor, Robert Yero, assistant bureau chief of District 3.

In a phone interview, Yero praised Lieb for her easy transition from being manager of Silver River State Park to managing both areas under Silver Springs State Park.

"Obviously, her workload increased significantly," Yero said. "With that transition came numerous tasks and a lot of things happening very quickly.

She did a phenomenal job. She's been able to bridge many relationships between contractors and employees, and she's brought in an army of volunteers to help manage all that."

Lieb, however, insists it is a shared award.

"To me, it's a recognition of everybody, the staff and the volunteers who worked so hard to prepare the park so we could open on Oct. 1 as a state park and feel some pride of what we had to offer," she said.

And the work goes on

While several dilapidated structures are coming down and animal enclosures are being eliminated, the Twin Oaks Mansion will remain for events and activities, and the Town Center will keep its row of restaurants and shops, Lieb said.

"It's a beautiful place to come and spend time," she said. "That's going to be the focus of our concessionaire, Silver Springs Management. They're making it possible for us to have the food service in place and the glass-bottom boats operating, and the kayak launch, which was ready right from the beginning. It's a really good mix of wanting to have exciting things for people to do but also protecting the resources."

Along with renovations of existing buildings and a restoration of the grounds, Lieb also oversees hiking trails, cabins and camp sites. She also has planned a variety of educational programs. In addition to guided walks and guided canoe trips, park rangers will give talks to visitors, she said.

The former park operator, Palace Entertainment, agreed to pay $4 million to get out of its contract and let the state take over. That money, Lieb said, has covered a good bit of the work; however, there are additional needed projects, such as reducing some areas of the parking lot that have a pervious surface and installing a grass lot for additional parking.

As for the Wild Waters water park, Lieb said, "It's up in the air right now." "Being the person on the ground, I'm not feeling comfortable with it right now," she said. "We're still trying to figure out if it's structurally sound and safe to operate."

Other plans include formation of a 2-mile hiking trail that will connect the springs side with the river side. A new boardwalk that meets ADA standards will lead to Ross Allen Island, where interpretive kiosks will memorialize the historic significance, as they already do in other locations in the park.

Hopefully, the artificial enhancements and midway rides won't be missed, Lieb said.

"People always want more, but they're ignoring what's out there that's wonderful," Lieb said. "I'm all about nature and natural Florida wildlife. Right now, the park is being planted with natural Florida vegetation. We have a mission statement that says, 'Providing recreation, but also preserving the resource.' We take all that into consideration. We will be so happy to have these new renovations. Then, we can enjoy the natural beauty of the park."

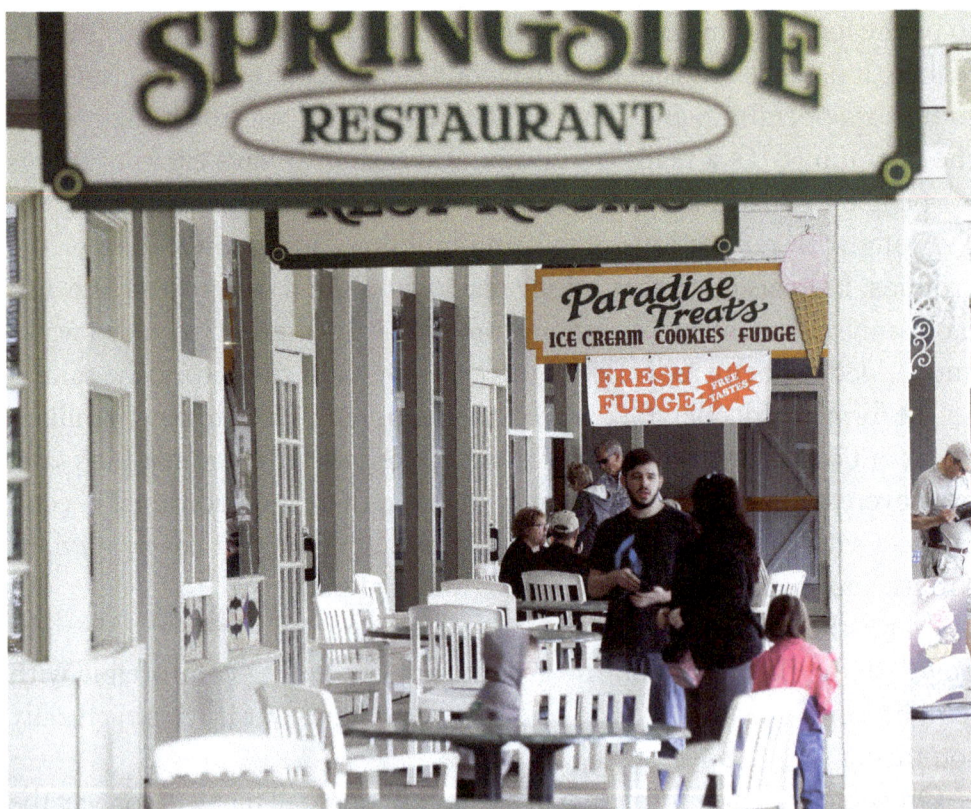

Restaurants have opened in Silver Springs State Park in Silver Springs, FL on Thursday March 27, 2014. The park is undergoing a restoration to a more natural state since the State of Florida Department of Environmental Protection took over the former tourist attraction in October. (Alan Youngblood/Ocala Star-Banner)2014

SPRINGS SCIENCE AND ADVOCACY

Robert L. Knight, Ph.D., Howard T. Odum Florida Springs Institute
(Reprinted from the Gainesville Sun, January 2018)

The Florida Springs Institute commends the efforts of the dozens of University of Florida research faculty and students who just completed a three-year study of Silver Springs and the Silver River. Tens of thousands of hours were spent on and under the cold spring water collecting information, and on computers analyzing the data and writing the 1,085-page final study report. After three years and roughly $3 million in state funding, UF has once again concluded that Silver Springs is experiencing excessive flow reductions and nitrate pollution.

Commissioned by the St. Johns River Water Management District in 2013, this scientific endeavor was initiated to learn more about the manageable factors that promote the growth of nuisance algae in Silver Springs. Numerous lines of investigation were pursued, and an encyclopedia of new data are now available that enhance understanding of springs ecosystem structure and function. For example, wildlife biologists found that alligators feed more on crayfish than on fish, with the lowly mudfish and gar feeding higher on the aquatic food chain. Ecologists found that filamentous algae overtaking springs are unpalatable by invertebrates that live in springs. Hydrologists determined that most groundwater discharging from Silver Springs flows through caves and underground conduits rather than through the rock matrix. Stream morphologists concluded that sediment deposits in the Silver River likely formed when the river channel was a quiescent lake rather than a mighty river. And, hydrologists confirmed that a long-term decline in flow velocity promotes a proliferation of filamentous algae in Silver Springs.

Project personnel at both UF and the St. Johns River Water Management District were divided into "super groups" and "research teams," basically isolated within their narrow research disciplines. Collaborative discussion was not encouraged. The basic question of what should be done to reverse statewide reductions in spring flows and increases in nitrate nitrogen pollution was not asked nor answered. In the process of conducting many dozens of individual experiments and measurements, there was no synthesis that recommended better management of springs by the water management districts or other state environmental protection agencies.

Dr. Howard Odum, a UF professor and the "Grandfather of Springs Ecology," described in 1957 the effects of industrial groundwater pumping on the death of Central Florida's Kissingen Spring. The Florida Springs Task Force formed by the Florida Department of Environmental Protection in 1999 called for a cap on groundwater pumping and limits on nitrogen loading from urban and agricultural fertilizers and septic tanks.

The Silver Springs 50-year retrospective study, funded by the state and conducted by UF, Wetland Solutions, and the District 14 years ago, found that depleted flow and elevated nitrate levels were causing significant and increasing ecological harm at Silver Springs. Multiple studies at Silver and Florida's other major springs by the Florida Springs Institute have further

Magic carpet ride through the previously healthy Silver Springs aquatic vegetation in 1956 (photo by Bruce Mozert, Florida Archives).

documented the widespread loss of spring health and outlined the steps needed for their recovery.

The specific actions that must be taken to save Florida's springs have been described repeatedly but apparently cannot see the light of day in Florida's political climate. After decades of credible evaluations of the problems ravaging Silver Springs, the St. Johns River Water Management District decided to reinvent the wheel by conducting another study, spending millions of dollars, and losing three more years of possible springs recovery time. The unstated purpose of this latest UF study was to delay taking any restorative action. Tragically, this tactic gave the District Governing Board the time and cover they needed to pass a highly flawed minimum flow rule and issue another groundwater pumping permit to Sleepy Creek that will result in further harmful flow reductions at Silver Springs.

For the past two decades the best science has told us that our springs will respond favorably to cutting back on groundwater extractions and reducing nitrogen loads to the land surface. But changing the status quo that protects Florida's land development and agribusiness profits is apparently taboo for the state's elected and appointed officials. Continuing to issue groundwater withdrawal permits and allowing more septic tanks is counter-productive to preserving Florida's springs. Without vocal outrage from voters, our leaders will continue to put business-as-usual over the best interests of the public.

ANIMALS FROM SILVER SPRINGS DISPERSED AS FAR AS ARIZONA

Story by Marian Rizzo/ Correspondent
(Reprinted from the April 12, 2014, article in the Ocala Star-Banner Newspaper)

There was a time when a 20-minute jungle cruise brought Silver Springs Attraction visitors eye-to-eye with water buffalo, zebras, gators and monkeys, a visit to Tommy Bartlett's petting zoo afforded a furry hands-on experience, and a stroll along flower-bordered paths took families to the far end of the park, where they fed wafers to giraffes and watched Kodiak bears loll in the sun.

Joanne Zeliff was introduced to such magical pleasures when she was 4 years old and took her first ride in a glass-bottom boat.

Jon and Cindy Johnson feed their goats and macaws at Johnson's Corner in Citra, Fla. on Wednesday, April 9, 2014. All of the animals except Baby Girl came from Silver Springs Attraction where Johnson worked for 21 years, first as a keeper, then as a lead keeper and finally as an animal supervisor. (Star-Banner Photo/Bruce Ackerman) 2014.

"Little did I know that I would one day work there for 33 years," said Zeliff, who started at the attraction in 1980 and moved up the ranks to become wildlife manager.

Zeliff left the park last July, a few months ahead of the transfer from Palace Entertainment to Florida State Parks. From January to June 2013, she had the final responsibility of finding new homes for 270 exotic animals.

"It was exhausting," she said. "A lot of zoos are limited for space, so it's hard to find homes. It was easier to get some of our animals to private places. If they were native animals of Florida, like birds of prey, we cannot sell them, so they would go through a transfer of permitting."

The first animals to leave were the otters, Zeliff said. Because they were hand-raised orphans, they couldn't be released into the wild. They went to Emerald Coast Wildlife Refuge in Fort Walton Beach.

The cougars and bears found homes at Wild Animal Sanctuary, a 700-acre large carnivore retirement facility in Denver. Most of the alligators went to Alligator Adventure in Myrtle Beach, S.C. The white alligator went to Wild Adventures in Georgia. The crocodiles relocated to Phoenix to a private breeder who does educational programs. Birds of prey and several reptiles went to the Central Florida Zoo in Sanford. A couple of emus settled in at the Jacksonville Zoo. Except for the rhesus monkeys, which run wild in the Ocala National Forest, all the animals that thrilled passengers on the jungle cruise had been vacated in 2004, Zeliff said.

"The state made us get rid of them," she said. "Basically, they blamed our animals for polluting the river. That was a big, big ride in the park. It was a terrible loss. We got rid of 52 animals in two days. They went to a private dealer to keep for breeding or to find homes for them."

The two giraffes, Kimba and Khama, which Zeliff helped bottle raise as babies, died of old age at 30 and 26, respectively. Frank, the last Galapagos tortoise at the park, was over 90 years old when he died. He had lived there since Ross Allen had his reptile exhibit there, Zeliff said. Then came the final relocation project in 2013.

"I would say every keeper had a crying moment when the animals left," Zeliff said. "I'd tell a lot of the keepers, 'These are not our animals. You can't get attached to them.'"

Zeliff's words came back to haunt her when she released a family of gibbons to the International Primate Protection League in Summerville, S.C.

"We all cried when we had to take them off their display," Zeliff said. "We had to knock each one out to give them a physical before they could leave the state. When we put those gibbons in the car, I bawled my eyes out."

Zeliff recently went to visit the gibbons and took a special interest in one named Elizabeth.

"I raised her for nine months when she was a baby," Zeliff said. "The keepers there said she remembered me. When I walked towards her cage, she came over and put her back to me for me to groom her. They said she doesn't come up to strangers. I didn't know how emotional it would be for me to go up there, but when I left, I was very happy. The keepers are excellent, and it was a beautiful place for them to be."

James Judy, vice president of operations for Palace Entertainment, also felt satisfied with the placements. He said he received photos from the Denver sanctuary that took the bears.

"They look phenomenal," Judy said. "They have winter coats. They have a lot more room to run—700 to 800 acres. It looked like a perfect fit."

Dr. Suzanne Billiar was a staff vet at Silver Springs from 1991 to 1996 and stayed on as a vet-on-call after she opened All Pets Clinic in 1996. She did many of the physicals required for relocating the animals.

"What comforted me, I knew (Palace Entertainment) was not in it for the money," Billiar said. "The few animals that were sold were mostly placed in sanctuaries. If anything, they probably lost a lot of money because of the labor involved and the shipping. The company was very good at letting Joanne handpick the places where they went. Basically, the people that paid for it were the people that were leasing the park."

Billiar said that for years Silver Springs served as a rehabilitation refuge, with about 300 cases every year.

"There were many heartwarming experiences," she said. "When you work with the type of animals that were at Silver Springs, it is a privilege to have the opportunity to just touch and see them up close."

Billiar admits there are risks to working with exotics.

"You're talking about animals that are potentially very dangerous. Kodiak bears and alligators," she said. "Even the monkeys we were working on could slice open your finger. It always takes a group of people working together, not just the veterinarian. Some people get a thrill out of sky diving or driving a race car. I get a thrill out of getting to hold some of these species that someday will be endangered or no longer exist."

In the end, Billiar went home with three tiny muntjac deer and a Stanley crane that had survived when Hurricane Andrew wiped out the Miami zoo.

In some cases, former park workers were able to relocate with the animals they had cared for. Andrea Junkunc, a wildlife employee there for 13 years, followed 14 birds of prey, a deer and several snakes to the Ellie Schiller Homosassa Springs Wildlife State Park.

Now the park services specialist at Homosassa Springs, Junkunc said she continues to work the birds of prey performances. While Silver Springs had a large outdoor arena with bleachers, Homosassa Springs has a smaller semi-indoor theater.

"We've taken some of the owls from Homosassa Springs and owls from Silver Springs and put them together in one program," Junkunc said. "At Silver Springs we had big productions with birds flying and showing very dynamic behaviors. Here, we take it a little bit slower and focus on conservation. We tell why they are living in captivity, what are their injuries, and how we can protect them in the wild. When the birds fly, we get them to the glove so there's more time for people to take pictures."

Local individuals who have the required state permits also have opened their doors to Silver Springs critters. Luis and Marcia Palacio, owners of Petting Zoo Ocala, acquired three llamas. One of the females had a hip injury and wouldn't eat and had lost some weight, Luis Palacio said.

"They had a severe problem with spitting," he added. "You couldn't come 10 feet near the male before he started spitting at you, like a machine gun. All our clothes are green from them spitting at us. We had to put on a mask and goggles."

Marcia Palacio said they trained the male to not spit by not irritating him. It was important to exercise patience and not react by getting mad, she said.

"Today, they're perfectly healthy and rehabilitated," Luis said. "Now we can approach the male and feed him by hand. And the one that was skin and bones has put on a little weight."

～

Cindy and Jon Johnson found room for several animals at their 18-acre farm in Citra.

Cindy, a Silver Springs employee for 20 years, took care of large animals, reptiles, primates and birds, and worked in the petting zoo. During her last six years, she was a supervisor of wildlife under Zeliff. When she left last June, Cindy brought home a cow, four goats, two macaws, a miniature donkey, two mini horses and a llama.

"When we brought them here they just stood in a corner," she said.

Joanne Zeliff, who was the wildlife manager at Silver Springs Attraction before it was taken over by the state last year, poses with a photo of herself bottle feeding giraffe Kimba in 1982, an ostrich egg and antlers from Axis Deer, at her home in northeast Ocala, Fla. on Monday, April 7, 2014. Zeliff relocated all of the exotic animals out of the park in 2013. Zeliff started working at Silver Springs on April 15, 1980 and rose in the ranks from animal keeper to animal supervisor to wildlife manager in 2013 when the privately owned park officially closed.
(Star-Banner Photo/Bruce Ackerman) 2014.

"They didn't know about trees. They didn't know about grass. Now they think they're in heaven."

To help the animals adjust, Jon built special enclosures for them.

As soon as she got the critters home, Cindy started introducing them to animals of the same breed. The cow, for example, was placed with a neighbor's herd.

"My neighbor told us the night he put her in there, she went out and tried to breed the bull," Cindy said with a laugh. "They spent the night in the pond, courting and smooching. It had been a long time since she'd been around anybody like herself."

"JACUZZI SPRINGS"

Robert L. Knight, Ph.D., Howard T. Odum Florida Springs Institute
(Reprinted from Gainesville Sun September 2018)

Nature's water cycle is amazing and free. Solar energy lifts fresh water from the ocean as vapor, transports it over the land with wind currents, and deposits precipitation on Florida at an average rate of about 150 billion gallons each day. About 15 billion gallons of this rainfall daily recharges the state's natural underground water storage and conveyance system. The remaining 90% evaporates or runs off in rivers to the ocean. This is like a natural Jacuzzi, bathing Florida's environment in life-giving freshwater at no cost.

Fast forward to 2018. Humans have corralled and re-directed Florida's natural water cycle to fulfill their own desires. Florida's surface water in rivers and lakes is widely impaired due to poorly regulated pollutant discharges and excessive withdrawals. Increasingly, Floridians have turned to underground waters for supply, first for drinking water and then for nearly every other use, including landscape and crop irrigation that was traditionally supported by rain.

The foreseeable consequence of this shift is the increasing depletion of Florida's most precious and least plentiful fresh water supply—the groundwater in Florida's aquifers. In north and central Florida, the resulting destruction of our natural springs and rivers that rely on groundwater inputs for dry-season baseflow is visible to all who care to look. Downstate in the absence of springs, aquifer depletion is harder to see.

Rather than facing this cascading calamity head-on by establishing a cap on groundwater pumping to reserve adequate water to protect natural environments, Florida's leaders continue to kick-the-can-down-the-road under cover of poor science and public apathy.

Some of us consume less than 30 gallons per day of groundwater for drinking, bathing, and cleaning and are content to rely on rain to water

The author's maternal grandparents, Nana and Pop-Pop Hines, at the Silver Springs Lucky Palm Tree in the 1950s. (family photo).

our grass. But the average Floridan consumes closer to 100 gallons per day of groundwater. Just by cutting out unnecessary water uses, we could reduce the public's 3-billion-gallon per day groundwater habit to less than 1 billion gallons per day.

Fortunately, a few areas of the state are concerned enough about depleted aquifers to have already cut historic water uses in half. Unfortunately, the benefits realized by this growing Florida water ethic are undone by a much smaller group of water users—namely for-profit business owners who shamelessly drink for free at the public water trough.

Water in Florida is a public trust resource, owned equally by all citizens. But, with no charge for using groundwater, the cunning few who control the water-permitting system easily gain permits to withdraw gigantic quantities of groundwater at no charge.

While water bottlers are a convenient target for public wrath about this corporate welfare, they are a literal drop-in-the-bucket compared to phosphate mines, paper mills, industrial farms, and others. More than 30,000 consumptive use permits allocate nearly half of all groundwater recharge in

Florida's Springs Region. Averaging more than 150,000 gallons per day each, these permits legalize groundwater extractions that are collectively killing our springs, arguably the most endangered natural landscape in Florida.

Despite compelling evidence that Florida's springs are drying up, the state's leaders continue to promote their costly charade justifying new water consumption permits based on obfuscation and flawed groundwater flow models. While restoring Florida's springs is as easy and free as reducing permitted groundwater allocations, the water management districts would rather bilk taxpayers for the cost of their own water.

For example, leaders at the St. Johns River Water Management District seriously considered putting a pipe in the Ocklawaha River downstream from Silver Springs and pumping the water to a treatment and recharge system next to the spring at an estimated capital cost of more than $100 million and annual operating costs of nearly one million dollars. District employees privately dubbed this ridiculous idea the "Jacuzzi Project."

Instead of cutting water use permits back in North Florida, the same water district is implementing a $40 million scheme to pump water from Black Creek to restore water levels in the Keystone area lakes. Once again, the cost for this Ponzi scheme will be borne by taxpayers rather than by the businesses who continue to profit by depleting the aquifer. A series of similar projects are in the planning stages in the Suwannee River Water Management District. Together these two water districts have projected a $300 million price tag to provide "alternative" water supplies to meet future demands.

The plethora of pump-treat-recharge projects being promoted by Florida's water managers is an embarrassment. How can these "public servants" continue to expend public money to implement these unnecessary water supply projects? The simple answer is that they are desperate enough to try anything to keep their jobs. If we don't demand better of our leaders, you can bet we won't get it.

MASSIVE FOSSIL COLLECTION SHARED WITH MUSEUM

Story by Marian Rizzo/ Correspondent
(Reprinted from the July 26, 2014, article in the Ocala Star-Banner Newspaper)

A fishing trip to Orange Springs in 1960 introduced Alvin Hendrix to a hobby that would take him on underwater treasure hunts for the next 40 years.

Hendrix and a friend were bringing their fishing boat to a pier on the Ocklawaha River when they encountered two men docking a boat. They were carrying scuba tanks and a piece of a mastodon tooth that caught Hendrix's attention.

In a Tuesday July 22, 2014 photo, Alvin Hendrix shows the first arrowhead he found when he began collecting from area rivers since the early 1960s in a storeroom at the Silver River Museum in Ocala, Fla. He donated those items to the museum where some are on display and others are tucked away in storerooms and vaults. Its now illegal to collect these items but wasn't at the time he began collecting. (AP PhotoOcala Star-Banner, Alan Youngblood)

"I was fascinated," he said. "I had grown up on that river, and I didn't know that kind of thing was there."

Before Hendrix could make a bid for the tooth, a bikini-clad woman came out of a nearby fish camp and asked if she could have it.

"The guy said yes and the lady took the tooth and left. That just shattered me," he said.

The incident motivated him to buy a wet suit and second-hand scuba gear, and he signed up for lessons at a Crystal River diving school.

After training, Hendrix went back to the place where he had seen his first mastodon tooth. What followed were a series of adventures at the bottom of a half-dozen North Central Florida rivers, where he collected thousands of historic and prehistoric artifacts.

Among Hendrix's finds were spear tips, mammoth teeth, mastodon jawbones, a variety of tools once used by Native Americans and the bones of many animals.

Earlier this week, a smiling Hendrix showed off some of the treasures he has collected at the Silver River Museum, where his donations number more than 16,000 items, many displayed in glass-fronted cabinets or placed on shelves in the classrooms where children come on field trips to learn about Florida's history.

To Hendrix, 81, the best use of such treasures is sharing them with youngsters.

"It's a thrill," he said. "I used to make speeches to the children's classes. It's satisfying when the children take an interest in something they never heard of before."

Scott Mitchell, museum director, touted Hendrix's donation of all the items as "one of the more important private artifact and fossil collections in Florida."

"Alvin explored the rivers of North Florida with scuba equipment during the '60s and '70s, long before most people knew that the bottoms of these rivers were full of treasures, such as prehistoric stone tools and ice age fossils," Mitchell noted.

"He also collected just about everything, including broken items, which gives us a very complete picture of the history of these areas in Florida. Many of his objects are on display, and all of them are available to researchers and people interested in the prehistory of North Central Florida," Mitchell added.

Hendrix's collection recently caught the eye of researchers who came to Ocala to study mammoth kill sites on the Silver River.

Morgan F. Smith, a candidate with the Center for the Study of Early Americans at Texas A&M University, said Hendrix directed the group to sites where he found artifacts. They also toured the museum.

"Alvin's collection is a really phenomenal representation of the cultural diagnosis of the Paleo-Indian in Florida," Smith said. "It's really important in archaeology to be able to work with people who have collections like Alvin's. When you get a collection that large, you can find out all kinds of things. The thing about Alvin is, he's so open. He's been very forthcoming about where he found everything, which is the way scientists and collectors should communicate."

Attention to detail

From the time he started collecting, Hendrix spent long hours numbering and categorizing each item, noting when and where they were found and what they likely were used for. He first stored the treasures in orange crates and shoved them underneath his house.

Hendrix said he received encouragement from many professionals, among them Barbara Purdy, retired professor of anthropology at the University of Florida and former curator in archaeology at the Florida Museum of Natural History.

In a phone interview, Purdy said most amateurs fail to keep the detailed records Hendrix has.

"Alvin's collection was so well-documented, I really learned a lot by studying it," Purdy said. "Because of my interest in prehistory, I was interested in his stone tool collection. I think what made Alvin make his final decision to give most of his collection to the Silver River Museum (is that) he was living in Marion County, and they were willing to take it and catalog it. It's where it should be."

In recent years, the cataloging fell to museum volunteer Monty Pharmer and his wife, Martha. Pharmer, 81, a retired Air Force pilot, puts in 20 to 30 hours every month at the museum. About 75 percent of his time is dedicated to Hendrix's collection.

"They asked me if I'd be interested," Pharmer said. "I jumped at the opportunity.

While we were doing that large collection we did the computer work at home. My wife helped me immensely. We sorted the collection and put the information in the computer, so it's easily available to researchers. They are not only important to the Silver River Museum, it's an important bunch of Florida artifacts that date back to historical times and help to understand early Florida."

Guy Marwick, executive director of the Felburn Foundation, founded the Silver River Museum in 1991 and served as its director until 2004. Marwick also noted the importance of Hendrix's detailed numbering system.

"It tells a better story about what may have happened, who may have lived there, and what time periods are represented in that area," Marwick said. "It's a tremendous collection. I mean, what kid doesn't want to find a mastodon's tooth or a mammoth's tooth? Alvin never lost that passion."

A thrilling hobby

Born in 1933 in a home in McIntosh, Hendrix spent part of his boyhood scavenging for relics among the groves in Orange Springs. After graduating from Reddick High School in 1951, he put in several years at UF, but his college education was interrupted when he was drafted into the U.S. Army during the Korean War.

Afterward, Hendrix returned to UF and earned a bachelor's degree from the College of Pharmacy. In 1962, he returned to his hometown and opened a pharmacy. Hendrix lost his wife, Juliette, to cancer 15 years ago, and he retired 10 years ago.

Looking back on what he considers the greatest hobby a guy can have, he talked about some of his most memorable adventures.

"The first time I went to Sunday Bluff, about five or six miles upstream from Eureka, I found 300 pieces," Hendrix said, his voice filled with excitement. "No one had ever been there. The water was clear and running fast. I was just picking them up off the top of one another. Two hundred of them were broken, but we found 100 complete. There was some beautiful material—bones and chert."

Most of Hendrix's dives were in shallow, clear water, but he also found objects in fields, in burial mounds and along shorelines. Some items were given to him by other divers. But, to him, the greatest thrill is scouring a river-bottom and coming up with your own find.

"There's actually a tool named after me," he said. "It's called a Hendrix scraper. It's a tool Indians used to scale fish."

Then, there were the deep rivers, like the St. Johns, where Hendrix would go down about 20 feet where it was pitch black. He rigged his own lighting system using a lawn mower battery and an aircraft landing light, and attached it to his weight belt with duct tape.

Hendrix said he would spend up to seven hours a day underwater, gathering everything from stone tools and glass bottles to animal bones and conch shells. There were disappointing times when he spent all day searching and came up with nothing.

"It's what we called bombing out when we didn't find anything," he said. "Sometimes, the water was too murky; sometimes there was too much silt."

Though Hendrix has given away most of his artifacts, he has kept a few treasures that sit in a pile on his grandfather's roll-top desk.

Laws now restrict people from taking such things from Florida's rivers, but Hendrix believes some leeway should be given to professionals.

In a Tuesday July 22, 2014 photo, Alvin Hendrix shows a knife blade along with some of the 16,000 prehistoric items he collected from area rivers since the early 1960s in a storeroom at the Silver River Museum in Ocala, Fla. He donated those items to the museum, where some are on display and others are tucked away in storerooms and vaults. Its now illegal to collect these items but wasn't at the time he began collecting. (AP PhotoOcala Star-Banner, Alan Youngblood).

"They've got to make a distinction between looters and legitimate anthropologists," he said. "It's a good law, because people were going out and selling these things on Craigslist. We don't know where they're going. We want to keep them in Florida."

THE OCKLAWAHA'S LOST SPRINGS

Robert L. Knight, Ph.D., Howard T. Odum Florida Springs Institute
(Reprinted from the Gainesville Sun, October 2019)

One or more Florida legislators, yet unnamed, have the enviable opportunity to undo the tragic mistake of a previous generation and be lauded as Florida Springs Champions. With bipartisan support in the house and senate appropriations committees, these champions are uniquely positioned to convince the 2020 legislature and Governor DeSantis to do what no other legislature/governor in the past 50 years has been willing or able to do—restore the 20 Lost Springs of the Ocklawaha River.

In 1971, a geology doctoral student at the University of Florida, Elizabeth Abbott, published a white paper titled "Twenty Springs of the Oklawaha [sic]". Described as "crystal pools," these limestone, artesian groundwater springs, in combination with Orange Springs, were estimated to add about one-third of the flow of the Ocklawaha River before it enters the St. Johns below the Rodman Pool.

The largest of these Lost Springs in terms of flow and surface area was Marion Blue Spring, privately owned but open to all for recreational pursuits, including fishing and swimming. Historically, Blue Spring emptied to the Ocklawaha River via Indian Creek, a five-mile clear spring run, just upstream of the current location of the Rodman Dam. Based on old-timer interviews, Dr. Abbott claimed that "the most discriminating of seasoned fisherman marveled at the 'quality' of fish at Blue Spring not to mention the 'quantity,'" and that "freshwater mullet and catfish swam like giant denizens convoyed by nervous bream, but the large bass was the most sought-after catch."

She finished her description of Blue Spring with these words, "gone is the blue crystal pool and the jet-mirror stream, replaced by dead vegetation and murky water."

Flooded by the artificial impoundment called the Rodman Pool, Blue and the other springs with names like: Bright Angel, Catfish, Cedar Landing, Sims, Bud, Mullet Cove, Indian Bluff, Tobacco Patch, and Cannon, have been lost for 50 years since the 1968 closing of the Rodman Dam as part of the ill-advised Cross-Florida Barge Canal. Only visible intermittently when the State of Florida draws down the level of water held in the Rodman Pool to flush massive rafts of rotting vegetation downstream to the St. Johns River, the uncovered springs of the Ocklawaha were compared to "blue eyes" peering skyward from the Floridan Aquifer by noted river guide and Florida author, Lars Anderson.

The historical and environmental significance of the Ocklawaha cannot be esteemed too highly. Site of numerous prehistoric mounds and archaeological sites; popular 19th century inland steamboat route to the heart of Florida's wilderness; and recipient of clear groundwater inflows from the world's historically largest, and best-known Silver Springs; the Ocklawaha is the largest tributary to Florida's longest and most commercially important river—the St. Johns.

Agnew's still on Silver Run c 1880. Featured in Margorie Kinnan Rawlings' book "South Moon Under", early Florida pioneers or "crackers" earned cash money distilling corn whiskey using water from the natural springs feeding the Silver and Ocklawaha rivers (Florida Archives.)

Through an inexplicable series of historical missteps and bad decisions, the living Ocklawaha and its precious springs have suffered some of the worst environmental depredations wrought by human civilization in North Florida. The only thing that is good about today's dammed Ocklawaha is that it can still be released from the "foot across her throat" as eloquently stated by another river guide and child of the river, Erica Ritter.

During the past 50 years, a long list of former Florida governors and senior agency staff have called for the restoration of the Ocklawaha River and springs. But, in an unfathomable twist of modern society, the will of these powerful leaders has been stymied by a small but vocal group of bass fishermen that oppose restoration.

Breaching the antiquated barge canal dam and returning the river to its natural channel is not only the most cost-effective future for the river, but is most beneficial with regards to downstream water quality and water quantity, regional economic benefits, public use of the river for recreational boating and fishing, and the ecological health of the St. Johns, Ocklawaha, and Silver Rivers.

Ocklawaha restoration is clearly in the public's interest and inevitably will be part of Florida's future. The only question that remains is who in Florida's government will open those "blue eyes" and be the river's champion?

A FAMILY LEGACY
RELATIVES OF LOCAL HERPETOLOGIST HOLD REUNION

Story by Marian Rizzo/ Correspondent
(Reprinted from the October 20, 2014, article in the Ocala Star-Banner Newspaper)

A family legacy came alive at the Silver River Museum over the weekend during a reunion of descendants of the late Ross Allen, Silver Springs' famed herpetologist who could stare down a rattler, overpower anacondas and dance around a pit of baby alligators, most of the time without a scratch on him.

From 1930 until 1965, Ross Allen ran the Ross Allen Reptile Institute, a favorite draw for tourists at Silver Springs Attraction, Ocala's historic theme park.

Director Scott Mitchell introduces guests to the museum's fossilized mammoth during the Ross Allen Family Reunion at Silver River Museum Saturday, Oct. 18, 2014 in Silver Springs, Fla. Family members came from as far as Alaska to celebrate the famous American herpetologist and collector and appreciate the memorabilia from his life. (Amy L. Stuart/Special to The Ocala Star-Banner)

Nostalgic stories filled the museum Saturday morning as Allen family members reminisced over black-and-white photos, brochures and news articles, plus technical papers written by Ross Allen and his longtime secretary, Everna Phillips.

The three-day reunion was organized by Robert Allen, the second of Ross Allen's biological children and his oldest son. The gathering drew more than 70 relatives from across the United States and from as far away as Alaska. Ross Allen's children, stepchildren, grandchildren and their in-laws enjoyed a Friday evening barbecue, a Saturday morning museum tour and boat rides on the Silver River, plus a Sunday morning service.

Betty Allen Bashaw, the eldest of the Ross Allen children, drove from Bradenton with her husband, Bill. The only daughter of Ross and Virginia Allen, Betty talked about what it was like growing up with three brothers. She said she learned how to catch baby alligators and she held indigo snakes so visitors could take pictures of them.

"I had to act like the boys," Betty said with a shrug. "I didn't mind that at all. It was exciting and educating. I never played with dolls, because I never had anybody to play dolls with. Our house was the nursery for animals that weren't big enough to put in the exhibit. We had baby alligators and baby otters in our bathtub—at different times, of course."

The beginning of a legacy

Born Jan. 2, 1908, Ross Allen was a native of Pittsburgh, Pennsylvania. His family moved to Winter Park when he was young. Allen developed a love of critters early in life. After one year of college, he dropped out of Stetson University to help support his family.

In 1929, when Silver Springs park was under the ownership of Carl Ray and W.M. "Shorty" Davidson, Ross Allen showed up with 22 snakes, $50 in cash and plans for a Florida reptile institute, which later became known as the Ross Allen Reptile Institute.

A self-taught herpetologist, Allen began his career with a taxidermy shop. His mother, Florence Martin Allen, was manager, while his brother, Oliver, helped with the expansion of the wildlife exhibit. They built pens and began stocking them with snakes, alligators, tortoises and other critters.

In time, Ross Allen constructed two demonstration arenas, put in a log cabin-style gift shop and eventually phased out his taxidermy business.

Aside from Tommy Bartlett's Petting Zoo and several boat rides, Ross Allen's shows were among the most popular attractions at the park.

Wide-eyed visitors sat in an outdoor arena and watched with open mouths as a trained handler flipped a baby alligator on its back and put it to sleep. Tourists jumped out of their seats when rattlesnakes popped balloons at lightning speed. The handlers gave an educational lecture while milking rattlesnakes, reserving the venom for medical labs to use for antivenin.

The bravest tourists would reach out and feel the hide of a baby gator, or they'd try to stand still for a photo with a boa constrictor draped around their shoulders.

Rarely was a handler bitten. Ross Allen himself suffered nearly a dozen bites from poisonous reptiles over the years. He survived two that were especially serious.

Craig Allen, son of Ross and his fourth wife, Jeanette, paused Saturday morning over a black-and-white photo of his father's blackened thumb, the result of a rattlesnake bite.

"He didn't lose his thumb," Craig said. "They made a spike out of it. It was really good for holding snakes, and if he put it under your collarbone, you quit misbehavin'."

Ross Allen's second near deadly experience happened while he was doing a venom extraction and a rattler bit into an artery just above the top of his boot.

"In about five minutes, he was totally paralyzed," Robert Allen said. "I was working at the museum in Gainesville at the time. I came down to visit him in the hospital."

Family ties

A charismatic athlete with steel blue eyes and a winning smile, Ross Allen married five times and had seven biological children and several stepchildren. Robert Allen recalled that each of his father's wives helped make the institute a success, either by organizing memorabilia, canning rattlesnake meat or traveling with him to South America on his "safaris."

Robert's mother, Virginia, worked in the gift shop and helped behind the scenes. After his parents divorced, Robert spent summer vacations with his dad. After graduating from high school, he worked full time at the institute, an experience that propelled him into a career working with young people at church camps.

"It was natural," Robert said. "Growing up working with animals was just something I enjoyed. Throughout all those years, even when I wasn't working for dad, I would go out snake hunting for him. My salary varied. Many snakes were $1 apiece. Rattlesnakes were $1 a foot. I called it making money, but we didn't even make enough to pay for the gas to bring them to him."

Robert described his dad as "a father of seven but a mentor to millions." "Through his work with summer camps, the Boy Scouts, and the Red Cross he touched many lives," Robert said. "He made education entertaining, and he worked to correct hundreds of common myths about snakes and other animals."

For Robert's brother, Tom Allen, the training went to unusual depths. A YouTube video from the 1960s shows the teenager and his dad tackling a giant anaconda. Tom took his experiences to another level when he later accepted a job as Marlin Perkins' co-host on *Mutual of Omaha's Wild Kingdom.*

"One of my first shows was on Ross Allen," said Tom. "It won an Emmy, so I had a job for the next 25 years."

To John Allen, there was nothing unusual about wading in the river, grabbing the snout of an alligator and lifting it out of the water with the help of his two brothers.

John was telling the story of how he took his wife, Sandy, alligator hunting on their first date, when a young boy walked into the museum.

"That may be one of ours. I don't know," John said, squinting. "This family's so big and the little ones keep coming."

Aside from mini gatherings, the last big reunion was held 10 years ago at Wakulla Springs, another of Ross Allen's favorite stomping grounds.

Craig Allen, son of Ross and Jeanette, traveled the farthest for Saturday's Ocala reunion. A captain with the Alaska State Troopers, he rallied 14 members of his family for the gathering. His brother, Kenneth, also lives in Alaska and was unable to make it. Their youngest brother, Sidney, lives in Georgia and was there with his family.

"I remember my dad was like a celebrity. So many people wanted to meet him and ask him questions," Craig Allen said. "As a child, I wanted to see what he was doing at the institute. For me, as a boy, it was a vast adventure to see the alligators and the snakes and ride the glass-bottom boat.

"The deer park was there. It was just every adventure you could imagine for a young boy," continued Craig. "Of course, we had snakes and alligators at home, too, so it was normal. It's what you grow up with."

The youngest visitor at Saturday's reunion was Craig Allen's grandson, 20-month-old William Ross Swanson. His mother, Terry, has been collecting Ross Allen memorabilia, including books and magazines, "and anything I can find on eBay," she said. "I found a can of the rattlesnake meat, and I have Ross' briefcase."

Beyond the family

In time, Ross Allen took over management of a Seminole village that was behind his institute. Several Seminole families lived there in thatch-roofed huts. They talked to tourists, carved dugout canoes and sold colorful handmade clothing.

Mary Billie Waggerby toured the museum Saturday morning and renewed old friendships. Waggerby said she was 4 years old when she first moved from Big Cypress Reservation in South Florida to Ross Allen's Seminole village.

Richard Fincher also was a young boy when he went snake hunting with his father, the late Dewitt Fincher, curator of the institute.

"All I can say is, it was extra money," Fincher said. "He'd pick up a snake and I'd say, 'Well, that's another $5 bill.'"

Lamont "Monty" Pharmer and his wife, Martha, have been longtime volunteers at the Silver River Museum. Monty said there was no end to the jobs a person could do, whether it was feeding the animals, cleaning the pens or hunting for critters.

"I looked forward to that little brown envelope each week," Pharmer said. "Working for Ross Allen also gave me permission to hunt the lands and swamp behind the institute. We all kept a pretty standard snake hunting array of equipment—a snake hook and a cloth dip net, and a snakebite kit."

Scott Mitchell, director of the Silver River Museum, conducted special tours for the family and also arranged for nostalgic boat rides on the Silver River.

"We were excited about the reunion, and we were happy to host it and make it enjoyable," Mitchell said. "This is the first time we've ever had a big reunion like this at the museum. Ross Allen was one of Silver Springs' main attractions. The park rangers have created a little museum center over there at Silver Springs.

There are quite a few pieces of Ross Allen memorabilia on display.

"The springs changed over the years dramatically," Mitchell added. "Up until the early 1920s, it was a riverboat and train hub and it was primarily commercial traffic. After Ross Allen came on the scene, it shifted to leisure and tourism. Ross Allen was part of what made it so successful. In a nutshell, he was in on the ground floor of making Silver Springs a tourist attraction. Many tourists wanted to come here just to see Ross Allen."

American Broadcasting Company took over operation of the park in 1962, and three years later, Ross Allen sold his exhibit to them and left the area. He had started building a reptile exhibit in Lake City when he was struck with cancer.

Ross Allen died at the age of 73 from a recurrence of cancer in 1981, while receiving treatment at Shands Hospital in Gainesville. His fifth wife, Gail Allen, was his caregiver until he died.

Craig Allen said he last visited Silver Springs in 2010.

"I showed my wife Ross Allen Island, especially where the institute was

A photograph of Ross Allen wrestling an anaconda is on display in the Ross Allen Reptile Institute display during the Ross Allen Family Reunion at Silver River Museum Saturday, Oct. 18, 2014 in Silver Springs, Fla. Family members came from as far as Alaska to celebrate the famous American herpetologist and collector and appreciate the memorabilia from his life.
(Amy L. Stuart/Special to The Ocala Star-Banner)

situated," Craig said. "We took one of the boat rides. The woman operator had been there since the 1970s, so I took the opportunity of telling her who I was. She was just thrilled that one of Ross Allen's sons was on her boat.

"She must have radioed ahead because wherever we went through the park, the staff came out, some so young they weren't even alive when my father was there," Craig continued. "They said they had heard stories about him and he was an inspiration for them. It's a very good feeling to know that there's a legacy still going on for my father so many years after he had done his work."

FLORIDA'S PADDLERS MUST UNITE

Robert L. Knight, Ph.D., Howard T. Odum Florida Springs Institute
(Reprinted from the Gainesville Sun, November 2018)

I recently had the good fortune to be invited to speak to the Florida Paddling Rendezvous at Silver Springs State Park. Hosted by the Villages Canoe & Kayak Club, this event has been held around the state for the past 15 years. At 446 members, The Villages has one of the largest paddling clubs in the state. More than 200 enthusiastic paddlers gathered at Silver Springs to dip their paddles in four spring-fed waterways: the Silver River, Ocklawaha River, Rainbow River, and Juniper Creek. Twenty-eight guided outings were offered during the three-day event and most attendees completed between three and four paddling trips (including night excursions on the Silver River), with trip distances ranging between six to ten miles.

The event was flawlessly orchestrated by volunteers from the Villages Canoe & Kayak Club. The entire state park campground was occupied by paddlers, as were dozens of surrounding motel rooms. While some meals were included in the registration, many visitors dined in local restaurants, spent money on transportation and other supplies, and paid park entry fees to state and local governments. An estimated $40,000 was infused into the Marion County economy from this one weekend of paddling. Paddlers came from all regions of Florida and from at least five other states, including California.

Best of all, paddling sports exert a minimal footprint on the natural water systems they visit. Paddlers take only pictures, kill only time, and leave no trace as they glide over the water surface. They do not scar the river bottom, damage the vegetation, or subject wildlife and fellow humans to noise pollution. Paddling a canoe, kayak, or paddle board provides an excellent opportunity to leisurely see and appreciate wildlife and natural plant communities, and to leave them almost untouched in their natural splendor.

Florida is home to the 1,515-mile Florida Circumnavigational Saltwater

Paddling Trail, as well as 57 inland water trails that include hundreds of miles of spring runs, rivers, lakes, and estuaries. Over 40 communities in 15 counties have earned the designation as "Paddling-Friendly Destinations." The 501(c)(3) non-profit Florida Paddling Trails Association has a host of "trail keepers" and "trail angels" who maintain trails and help paddlers utilize this Florida Blueway network. The diversity and majesty of Florida's

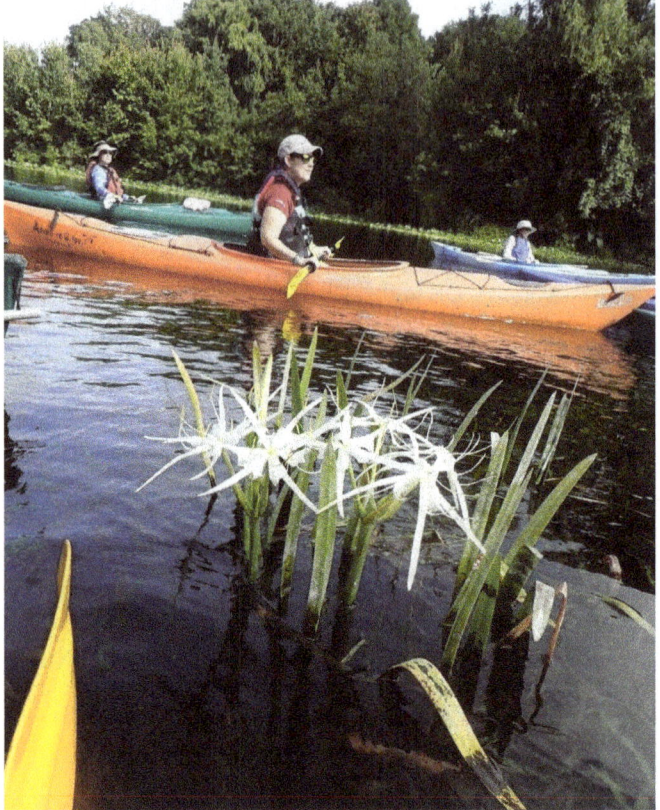

Kayakers on the Silver River with native spider lily in foreground in 2019 (photo by author).

paddle trails is legendary throughout the U.S.

There are currently no estimates of either the number of non-motorized watercraft in Florida or the number of residents and tourists who annually enjoy these sports. But anyone who visits popular inland and coastal waterways can see that the number of people utilizing non-motorized watercraft is growing by leaps and bounds. Currently in Florida there are hundreds of thousands if not millions of individuals enjoying these nature-based recreational activities. The economic return from this dedicated and expanding group of paddlers is equally great.

And yet, the expansion of nature-based tourism in Florida is dependent on the continuing presence of abundant and clean natural waters. Paddling sports are not compatible with dying springs, stagnant rivers, shrinking lakes, and guacamole-filled estuaries. Florida's economy and future are inextricably linked to protecting and, in many cases, restoring our waterways. Too much has already been lost due to excessive groundwater pumping, discharge of nutrient-laden wastes, and lax enforcement of environmental laws intended to protect these natural treasures.

We have only ourselves to blame if we do not elect and hold accountable governmental officials to better protect our valuable natural resources. You the voter must be alert for election-day-environmentalists who hope to be re-elected, only to continue their real agenda of supporting developers and industries that prioritize short-term profits over the health of Florida's waters.

WOODEN GLASS-BOTTOM BOAT
STIRS MEMORIES OF SILVER SPRINGS

Story by Marian Rizzo/ Correspondent
(Reprinted from the June 4, 2018, article in the Ocala Star-Banner Newspaper)

Darrell and Jim Buchanan say their father and two uncles helped build and repair the wooden boats of the late 1940s.

While visiting a glass bottom boat display at the Silver River Museum complex recently, Darrell and Jim Buchanan looked through old photos and reminisced about a time, when, as youngsters, the two brothers spent summers at what is now Silver Springs State Park.

It was the late 1940s. Life was simpler back then. Entry was free,

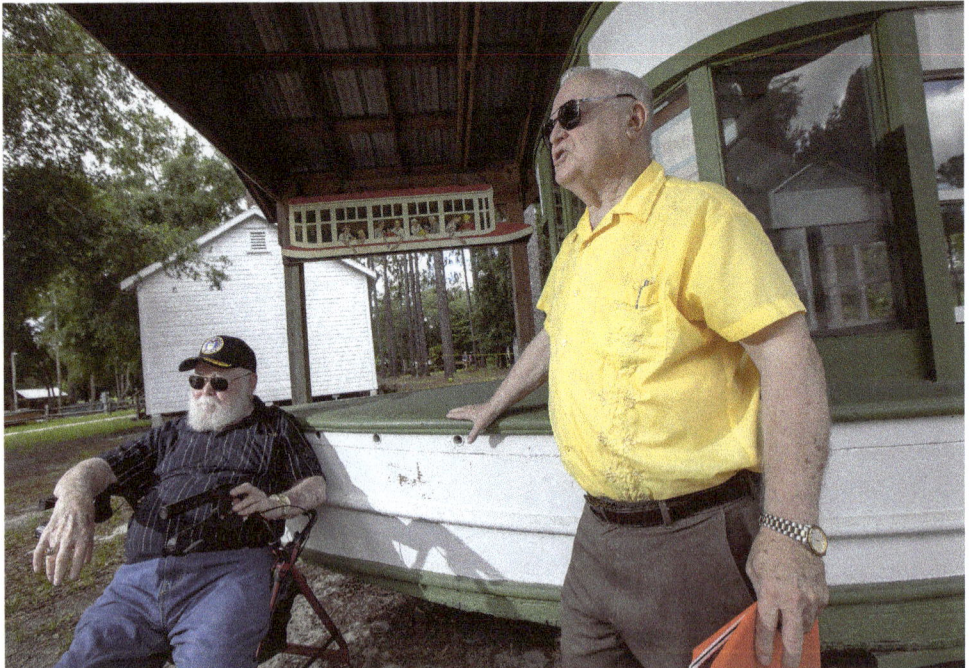

Jim Buchanan, left, and his brother Darrell Buchanan talk about hanging out with their father in the 1940s when he worked on Glass bottom boats at Silver Springs. They are shown near a restored boat from that era at the Silver River Museum in Silver Springs, Florida on Thursday May 31, 2018. [Alan Youngblood/Ocala Star-Banner]

and ABC Paramount had not yet turned the property into a for-profit playground.

The main attraction was the glass-bottom boats that gave tourists a crystal clear view of aquatic life at the bottom of the springs. And the Buchanan boys' father and two uncles were part of the work crew that built and repaired those boats.

Jim Buchanan, 81, was about 9 years old at the time. He described the experience as "magical."

The boys either went swimming or they toured the Seminole village at Ross Allen's exhibit, where their mother worked as a guide. They also spent time watching the men work on the boats.

"We would go down and they'd be laying the keel, or they'd be working on the outer structure," Jim said. "It took seven or eight months to put one together. Over a period of time, water got into the wood, or battery acid would leak out and would eat through the wood. The seats had to be sanded and varnished so people wouldn't get splinters from them."

All of the boats were given an Indian-themed name, such as Osceola or Seminole.

"When they christened them, they actually broke a bottle on them and gave them their name," Jim said.

Darrell Buchanan, 79, was 6 years old in 1945 when he first went to the park with his father, Elic Buchanan, and his uncles, Hugh MacManus and Archie Buchanan. Archie was foreman of the work crew, which also took care of the springs and did maintenance and electrical repairs throughout the park, Darrell said.

"In the summertime, we used to live at Silver Springs," he said. "It was heaven. We have fond memories of learning how to swim and just going back to the workshop and watching our dad and uncles do all kinds of work. It was great for a kid."

"I especially liked listening to the chimes," he added. "An organ player was hired to come in at the end of the day. Loudspeakers were up in the trees and chimes would go off all over the park."

During the 1950s, Silver Springs management started to phase out the wooden boats in favor of aluminum ones, said Scott Mitchell, director of the Silver River Museum and Environmental Education Center, which is a program of Marion County Public Schools.

"For a while, they ran both at the same time," Mitchell said. "Eventually, the pointy-prowed, wooden ones disappeared and they only had the flat-prowed, aluminum boats. It didn't happen overnight."

Guy Marwick, former director of the museum, mentioned Hullam Jones, a local man who came up with the idea of a glass-bottom boat in 1878. Jones inserted a pane of glass in the bottom of a dugout he built from scratch, Marwick said.

The concept caught on at Silver Springs, where construction of glass-bottom boats began in the 1920s or 1930s. Later, resorts in other parts of Florida began using them in such places as Key West and the Gulf of Mexico, where tourists continue to take excursions in watercraft that allow them to gaze into the depths without ever stepping out of a boat.

Silver Springs' original glass-bottom boats were scrapped or sold off. One ended up as a houseboat for a while and later was salvaged from the banks of the Ocklawaha River by Francis and Katherine Gay. The Gays donated the boat to the Silver River Museum in the late 1990s.

"To my knowledge it's the only one left of the earliest ones," Marwick said. "It went out of service many years ago. It was so primitive, the prow was pretty well split apart. A small kid could have walked out the front."

In an effort to have the boat restored, Marwick called on a retired handyman, Bob Butler, who also served as a volunteer at the museum for many years.

Butler agreed to take a look.

"It was in a huge shed on top of several 50-gallon drums," Butler said. "It had rotted to the point where it was questionable whether it was fit to present at the museum. Guy asked if I thought it was recoverable enough to show it. I said, 'I'll take a shot at it.' I didn't even know if it would hold together. It was a wreck."

The boat was transported to Butler's backyard, where it was placed on blocks.

"Here's this derelict boat sitting in my backyard with broken windows and screens and half a dozen mud dauber nests," Butler said. "It looked like a Disney idea for a haunted ship."

Butler worked on the boat every day for five or six weeks, painting, hammering and repairing wood. He also had to restore the curved mahogany benches where someone had spilled paint and tar. It was worth the effort, he said.

"This boat was the first one designed to be featured as a springs boat," Butler said. "Way back before that, you went out on a rowboat and they gave you a glass-bottom bucket to look in the water."

Butler said he spent $500 on supplies and, of course, his labor was free. When he finished, he phoned Marwick, and the boat was moved to the museum property and put on display inside a protective shed.

"I think it's really in a great spot," Marwick said. "A tornado went right over it and took out some trees, but the shed protected that boat. It wouldn't be there at all if it weren't for Bob Butler and the work he did. He really saved that boat. It's a valuable piece of history."

A 1940s era handout photo shows Jim Buchanan and his brother Darrell Buchanan's father working on a glass bottom boat. The men were children then and talk about hanging out with their father on glass bottom boats at Silver Springs. They are shown near a restored boat from that era at the Silver River Museum in Silver Springs, Florida on Thursday May 31, 2018. [Alan Youngblood/ Ocala Star-Banner]

A BRIGHT FUTURE FOR SILVER SPRINGS STATE PARK

Guy Marwick, Felburn Foundation and founder Silver River Museum
with Robert L. Knight, Ph.D., Howard T. Odum Florida Springs Institute

Proclaimed by a traveler in 1856 to be "… a grand hydrographical feature of North America ranked with Niagara Falls and the Mississippi River …," Silver Springs is the largest artesian spring in the United States. Centrally located in Florida and home to the state's first major tourist attraction, Silver Springs is a National Natural Landmark and is a premier destination for travelers worldwide.

Silver Springs is also the "Crown Jewel" of the Florida State Park System. Encompassing 4,660 acres and including the entire Silver River, Ocala's only state park was purchased to conserve the natural and cultural beauty of the area and to inform and educate the public. Development in the state park is limited to uses that are compatible with the mission and goals outlined by the Department of Environmental Protection's Division of Recreation and Parks.

In 2013 and 2014 when the Silver Springs and Wild Waters attraction was combined with the existing Silver River State Park, state officials hosted a series of advisory team meetings to identify specific uses that would or would not be compatible with park re-development. Removal of the dilapidated Wild Waters infrastructure was a priority for the state park. One proposed compatible use was inclusion of a new springs and freshwater science education and research facility. Demolition of Wild Waters provides an ideal space near the park's entrance for fulfilling this interpretive goal. Recently, the private, non-profit Howard T. Odum Florida Springs Institute has been encouraged by the Florida Park Service to develop a proposal to establish the Silver Springs Environmental Institute.

The proposed Silver Springs Environmental Institute would include education and interpretive experiences for all ages. The new institute would house a series of displays describing Florida's rich springs diversity, including their hydrology, chemistry, biology, and cultural resources. The springs institute would also include a research laboratory to support ongoing monitoring of Florida's artesian springs, and classrooms and boating access for researchers and student interns. The proposed Silver Springs Institute would be designed to augment and enhance the existing Silver River Museum that focuses on elementary school students.

The Silver Springs Environmental Institute would collaborate with educators and researchers from state universities, community colleges, advanced high school programs, state and local agencies, and non-profit scientific organizations. This facility would accommodate visiting students and faculty and provide a new center for scientific excellence in Marion County. Area businesses, including lodging, food, and entertainment would benefit economically from the increased flow of visitors and professionals attracted by the proposed Silver Springs Environmental Institute.

To facilitate access to the vast network of trails and public lands radiating out from Silver Springs and the Cross-Florida Greenway, this proposed re-development plan would provide space for compatible concessionaires, such as outdoor adventure gear sales, and bicycle and kayak sales and rentals. Visitors would have several choices when they enter park property from SR 40. They would be able to start their visit with no charge at the aesthetically-designed Silver Springs Environmental Institute to get an overview, maps, equipment, and background on park amenities; enter the head spring attraction area by paying standard admittance fees; or head straight for the canoe/kayak concession to immerse themselves in the Silver/Ocklawaha Blueway.

A key concern of the park advisory committee in 2014 was the documented decline in Silver Springs due to flow reductions and increasing groundwater pollution. The proposed Silver Springs Environmental Institute would have the in-house expertise to champion springs restoration and protection. When interviewed by the *Ocala Star Banner* in 2013, the former head of the Florida Park Service Donald Forgione stated that "Every one of our state parks is special. But Silver Springs is going to be the most unique and special among them." He added, "It's not going to be a terrific park if it isn't terrific environmentally."

The education and research benefits provided by locating the proposed Silver Springs Environmental Institute at Silver Springs State Park would help to ensure the restoration and protection of this world-class natural wonder. The benefits to the residents of Silver Springs, Ocala, Marion County, and to all the people who reside in or visit Florida, will be immense.

Proposed Silver Springs Environmental Center by the Howard T. Odum Florida Springs Institute to be located on the former site of Wild Waters (concept by Kp studio architect).

A VISIONARY TALENT

Story by Marian Rizzo
(Reprinted by permission from the June 2020 article in Ocala Style Magazine)

Anybody who ever stepped inside Bruce Mozert's tiny studio in Silver Springs would have collided with hundreds of photos strewn across two desks and plastered on all four walls. Visitors walked among piles of crudely built waterproof camera housings, assorted pieces of inventions he hadn't yet figured out, and a filing cabinet crammed with negatives from his 30-year career as Silver Springs' official photographer.

Even in his mid-90s, Mozert perked up at the sight of a visitor coming through his door. The white-haired champion of underwater photography instantly morphed into a younger version of himself as he reminisced over the high points of his career. His eyes sparkling, he'd sit on a rolling chair and pass from one artifact to another, showing off the numerous contraptions that made him an icon of his time.

Mozert died on October 14th, 2015, just a few weeks before his 99th birthday, leaving behind a legacy of photos, negatives and inventions. A couple of years later, the long process of sorting through Mozert's treasure trove began, with several people—who found themselves amazed by the scene—showing up to help.

Bruce Mozert shown with his camera
Photo courtesy of Evelyn Yorlano.
Used here by permission of Ocala Style Magazine.

Among them, Alan Youngblood, an accomplished underwater photographer in his own right, was astounded by what he uncovered. Some of Mozert's early inventions had crude beginnings, fashioned from scrap metal, Plexiglas, soldering wire and rubber inner tubes, but they worked. Back in Mozert's day, photographers didn't have the high-tech equipment that's available today.

"When they got into the business, they had to make everything," Youngblood notes. "Today, when I'm photographing underwater, I'm literally standing on the shoulders of giants and Bruce Mozert is one of them. I get to dive with state-of-the-art modern equipment. He didn't have any of that and he made beautiful pictures. He had the right attitude for anyone in the business. If someone asked him to do something, he said, 'Sure,' and he'd figure it out later. He pioneered underwater photography."

As a photojournalist, Youngblood photographed Mozert a number of times.

"There was always plenty of chitchat," Youngblood recalls. "He would answer whatever you asked him. He talked to me a little bit about filtering, and he pointed out the value in thinking through a problem and developing whatever you needed to do to accomplish it. That skill has served me not only in photography, but in anything that I do."

Esteemed local natural history photographer Mark Emery also holds Mozert in high regard.

"He absolutely solved a problem nobody else could solve," Emery remarks. "He found a way to do it. He was involved in making a photo boat with a glass bottom and 6-foot glass case all around. You could walk down steps and now you were six feet below the water. It was an amazing way to see the Silver River, like a diver would see it, at least the first couple layers."

Often surrounded by beautiful young women, Mozert considered them pleasant-looking props, no different from photographing a two-by-four piece of wood or a dilapidated stove he'd somehow managed to sink to the bottom of the main spring.

He directed his bathing beauties in a variety of poses—standing on tiptoe to emphasize the sleek lines of their legs, shooting up at them to make the shorter ones appear taller, and placing them underwater, cooking on a grill, lounging in a lawn chair, playing golf and being hauled off by a sea monster.

Such was the fate of Ginger Stanley Hallowell who was the stunt swimmer in *Creature from the Black Lagoon* and its sequel, *Revenge of the Creature*. She also posed for many of Mozert's advertisement photos that promoted the films and Silver Springs as a tourist attraction.

Now 88 years old and living in Orlando, Hallowell recalls that Mozert showed total respect for all of his models.

"He appreciated the fact that we looked good and that he could photograph us, but at the same time it was almost like we were inanimate objects, like a doll that he could pose. He was a total gentleman."

All the while, Mozert's mind was on the next project.

"You could always see the wheels turning." Hallowell laughs. "Many times, he'd get ahead of himself. He would say, 'Hey, I think we can do an underwater circus and we can get NBC here and I can make all the props. We can have a snack stand with a canopy over it and we can get one of Ross Allen's snakes and you can be a snake charmer.' There was always a twinkle in his eyes, because he always had a thought. His expression would change, and, in his mind, he would go through the whole little short subject that he was going to put you in. He had already seen the end, and the end was always a comedy or a surprise.

"One time, we took an old jalopy down in the water, along with a picnic basket and a tablecloth, and we spread out an underwater picnic," Hallowell recalls with a giggle. "We actually got in the car as it rolled down the bank and into the water. It was very unusual and kind of fun."

One of Hallowell's scenes in *Creature from the Black Lagoon* involved an unplanned swimming "dance" she did with underwater Creature double Ricou Browning.

Now 90, Browning, of Fort Lauderdale, has fond memories of working at Silver Springs, like the time he and Mozert set up an underwater radio station that really worked.

"One time, Ginger swam the whole length of the Silver River underwater," Browning remembers. "Bruce filmed it and I was there just giving her air. She stayed underwater several miles, all the way to the end."

Mozert didn't start out with a camera in his hand. Born on November 24th, 1916, in Newark, New Jersey, he moved with his family to a chicken farm in Scranton, Pennsylvania. After graduating from high school, he took a job driving a coal truck. Not one to sit still for very long, he followed his sister Zoe, a professional model, to New York City where he began working as a film developer for *LIFE Magazine*, earning $3 a week.

In 1938, while in Miami on an advertising shoot, Mozert heard a movie studio was about to shoot a series of *Tarzan* movies at Silver Springs. He dropped what he was doing and came to Ocala. Media personality Buddy Martin was just 3 years old when he met Mozert.

"My dad, Wilton Martin, was the first public relations director at Silver Springs," notes Martin. "He actually brought Bruce to Ocala. I remember Bruce coming to our house and setting up his darkroom in our bathroom. I remember going in the bathroom and seeing strips of film hanging on our shower curtain. My dad was the one who pushed Bruce to invent the underwater camera."

During his career as Silver Springs' official photographer, Mozert rubbed elbows with numerous stars who came to town with Hollywood filmmakers. His collection of photos includes shots of Gregory Peck, Lloyd Bridges, Esther Williams and a host of others. Mozert's work appeared on the covers of major magazines, and his movie shorts were shown in news clips that played before feature films at movie houses across the nation. One of them, a Thanksgiving dinner with a real turkey eaten underwater, made it to the big screen every November for a few years.

But Mozert's life wasn't all work and no play. Ryan Mozert, who lives in Gainesville, says whenever he spent time with his grandfather they got away from the studio and did other things, like fishing trips to Cedar Key with Ryan's brother Clint, and their dad, Scott Mozert.

"I worked with Bruce all the way up to two weeks before his death," reminisces Ryan. "We went to the lake, setting up a satellite, picking up branches, painting. He taught me how to fix jet skis and outboard motors. He was great, very loving and had a good business sense about him. He was a Christian. He belonged to the Lions Club and used to fix bicycles and give them to homeless people."

As for Mozert's collection, after his death it fell into the hands of Evelyn Yorlano, his "girl Friday" for 38 years.

"He never threw anything away," Yorlano sighs. "His mind was always going 100 miles an hour, thinking how he would make something or fix something."

As executor of Mozert's estate, Yorlano kept the office open until his estate was settled and the collection ready for another home. In desperation, she enlisted the help of local journalist and photographer Dave Schlenker.

Schlenker had a professional and a personal relationship with the man he describes as "an icon of photography."

"When I was in photo school, I needed a large format camera," Schlenker recalls. "I didn't have access to one, so I called Bruce up to find out where I could get one. He said, 'Meet me at my studio.' He had a large format camera there. He said, 'Take it for as long as you need it.' That camera might have photographed Jayne Mansfield and underwater alligators! I got to use it until I finished school."

Schlenker was not prepared for the "treasures" inside Mozert's tiny studio.

"The place was like a completely disorganized wonderland," Schlenker says, chuckling. "He was a bit of a pack rat. We were going through these filing cabinets and finding these iconic images—Jayne Mansfield shoved in there next to a reptile show, aerial photos of Weeki Wachee, Cypress Gardens and Silver Springs, starlet photos in bikinis, Ross Allen—and there's Bruce's wife waving and with a suitcase on vacation. I thought, This stuff needs to stay in Marion County."

He contacted Dr. James Henningsen, president of the College of Central Florida, who arranged a partnership between the college, Marion County and the Florida Division of Cultural Affairs. Together, they bought the collection for $85,000. The majority of artifacts went to the state museum archives in Tallahassee, and a portion remained in Marion County.

"The nice thing about this agreement, it preserved [the collection] for Florida's history, and made it available to the public," Henningsen states. "We have a number of originals that were colorized and framed. They're housed at the Appleton. We would like to display some of those on campus and rotate them."

Six prints are currently on display in the lobby at the Ocala/Marion County Visitors and Convention Bureau. Jessica Marr, marketing and communications coordinator for tourist development, notes that Mozert has been nominated for admission into the Florida Tourism Hall of Fame. This year's recipient will be named at the Florida Governor's Conference on Tourism in September.

Mozert was posthumously named first inductee on Ocala's Walk of Fame on May 3rd, 2018. Prior to his death, he received a lifetime achievement award at the Silver Springs International Film Festival and also served on a panel with other filmmakers.

"He was such a storyteller," muses Angie Lewis, a board member for the festival. "I could listen to him for hours. His memory was phenomenal. He would rattle off dates and time periods and stories. It was just mesmerizing."

Among the other ways Mozert has been memorialized is through the pages of *Silver Springs: The Underwater Photography of Bruce Mozert*, published in 2008 by Gary Monroe. The hardcover book is filled with the images that put Silver Springs on the map, and helped him earn a place in history. Many of the images show model Betty Frazee Haskins, who worked with Mozert for about three years.

She says that in addition to the underwater images, he also created plenty of daring and creative setups on land.

"We made pictures in different venues, like the limestone pits up in Lowell," she recalls. "That was a magazine cover. I was sitting on the top of the cliff and Ricou Browning was doing a swan dive off into the water."

Bruce Mozert in Silver Springs with his underwater camera, circa 1950
Photo from the Bruce Mozert Collection, Florida State Archives.
Used here by permission of Ocala Style Magazine.

Some of the work was for advertising clients, or for businesses trying out new ideas.

"We did Mercury Motors, all their ads," Haksins offers. "And people were always testing products at Silver Springs, like Styrofoam, which was beginning to be widely used. They carved a mountain out of Styrofoam and I was on it in something like a red Santa suit and it was floating out in the springs."

"He was always thinking of something kitschy to do, and I worked in the PR department for Bill Ray," she remarks. "Whenever they had something

Bruce Mozert photographing a model underwater at Silver Springs in 1950.
Photo from the Bruce Mozert Collection, Florida State Archives.
Used here by permission from Ocala Style Magazine.

195

they wanted to do, they called me down and said, 'wear this or wear that.' I learned to do things like drinking a Coke underwater, eating a banana. All kinds of underwater stuff, but we did a ton of stuff above water too. Sometimes we'd have an animal; an elephant, a snake, a monkey."

Haskins says the publicity pictures went all over the world, and the picture of her cooking a steak underwater was on the cover of Smithsonian Magazine. Her photos graced the covers of 21 magazines, and she worked on sets for *Sea Hunt* and a Jerry Lewis movie.

"I was a teenager and pretty game for everything that went on," she offers. "Bruce was a very interesting man, very creative. He was always saying funny things, but he was dead serious about his work."

SILVER SPRINGS, HEAL THYSELF!

Robert L. Knight, Ph.D., Howard T. Odum Florida Springs Institute
(Reprinted from the Gainesville Sun, April 2019)

Medice, cura te ipsum! (physician, heal thyself!) is an applicable biblical quote depicting the current fate of Silver Springs. Attributed to Jesus in Luke 4:23, this passage can be interpreted to warn against the hypocrisy of claiming to have the ability to solve a problem in others while being unable to avoid the problem in ourselves.

In early 2018 the Florida legislature ratified Senate Bill 670, codifying a "prevention strategy" for Silver Springs. The purpose of this addition to the St. Johns River Water Management District's consumptive use applicant's handbook was … "to ensure that flows and levels within Silver Springs do not fall below the recently adopted minimum flows and levels (MFLs) during the next 20 years." The minimum average flow the District had recently adopted for Silver Springs was 412 million gallons per day (MGD) which authorized an average flow reduction of 22 percent compared to the historic, pre-1990 average Silver Springs flow of 530 MGD.

At the end of 2017 the annual average flow at Silver Springs was 301 MGD or 111 MGD below the "minimum" average set by the District and 43 percent (229 MGD) lower than the historic average. In fact, annual average flows at Silver Springs for 16 of the 18 years prior to 2017 had been below the minimum regulatory target. In the meantime, Silver Springs was visibly dying as evidenced by blue waters turning green, and the rampant, nutrient-fueled growth of filamentous algae and submerged aquatic vegetation. The intersection between rapidly rising nitrogen enrichment and declining flows was exceeding the capacity for Silver Springs to "heal herself."

Conveniently, Mother Nature came to the rescue with record rainfall totals in Marion and Alachua counties in 2017 and 2018. After hitting a daily low flow of 206 MGD in June 2017, Silver Springs flows began to rise as soon as the summer rains began. The 2018 rainfall continued strong with more than 125 inches of rain in the previous 19 months, raising Silver Springs' annual average flow above the District's minimum average for the first time in 13 years. But, even after two years of near-record rainfall, Silver Springs' flows were still well below historic wet year conditions.

On recent sampling trips to Silver Springs, staff with the Florida Springs Institute documented an amazing change. Large areas of the Silver River's bottom that had been covered by dense growths of noxious filamentous algae, now show their former white sand and shell sediments. Rising spring flows have resulted in higher water velocities, achieving the natural cleansing effect that occurred almost continuously before the 1990s. Over a large area Silver Springs is silver once again!

Other than the doubtful benefits of the District governing board's prayers for more rain, Mother Nature gets the kudos for this startling transformation. Under the cover of the flawed minimum flow rule the District continues to issue new groundwater pumping permits. Every new permit and pumped well draws more water from the Floridan Aquifer.

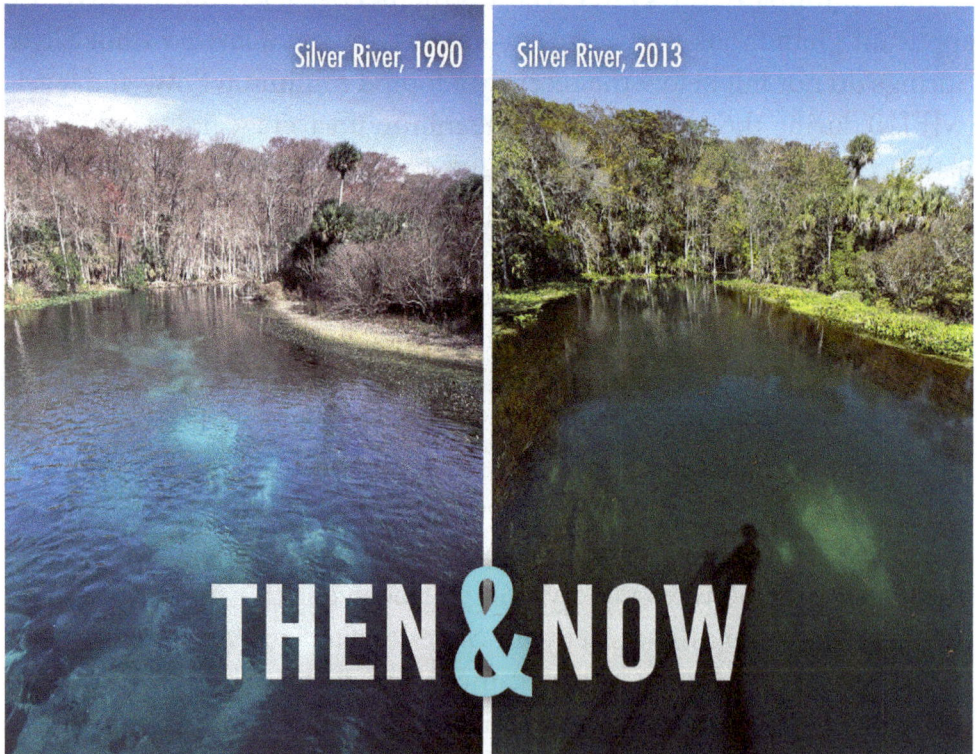

Before (1990) and After (2013) photos of the Silver River from the identical location (photos by John Moran).

Every new groundwater extraction further reduces the long-term average flow in Silver Springs.

Wikipedia defines hypocrisy as "… the contrivance of a false appearance of virtue or goodness, while concealing real character or inclinations; … hence, in a general sense, hypocrisy may involve dissimulation, pretense, or a sham." The St. Johns River Water Management District's Silver Springs' minimum flow rule is hypocritical and does not prevent the issuance of additional well permits that contribute to the drawdown evident in the Floridan Aquifer or the continuing decline in long-term average flows at Silver Springs.

Silver Springs cannot heal herself. As guardians of the public trust, it is our government's responsibility to act in the best interest of the people and prevent significant environmental harm. Most importantly, it is the government's responsibility to protect in perpetuity precious natural resources like Silver Springs.

AFTERWORD

Public vigilance and a healthy share of skepticism are the best protections against the continuing degradation of Silver Springs. True restoration of Silver Springs will likely require the following regional efforts:

- A permanent reduction of existing groundwater extraction throughout north and central Florida to less than 50 percent of today's rates;
- Elimination or major reduction of all urban/suburban uses of nitrogen fertilizers;
- An incentive-based program to shift agriculture from water and nitrogen-intensive crops to managed forests;
- Upgrades to all regional wastewater treatment facilities and replacement of many septic systems by central treatment facilities;
- Restoration of the Ocklawaha River to allow unimpeded migration of fish and manatees up the Silver River; and
- An informed and energized public that has easier access to Silver Springs through the new state park and the ability to recognize and oppose threats and celebrate successes.

This is an exciting time in the long history of Silver Springs. One of the wonders of the natural world, Silver Springs has the chance to turn the corner from more than 50 years of regulatory neglect and decline, to a future of recovery and protection. Silver Springs can serve as an allegory for all of Florida's natural wonders. Either it can go the way of the Ivory Billed Woodpecker and Carolina Parakeet or it can be returned from near extinction like the Brown Pelican and the Bald Eagle.

The future of Silver Springs is a choice that will be made by the actions or inactions of our generation.

FILM, TV, & COMMERCIALS

Many films and commercials were shot at Silver Springs during the attraction's glory days. The following is a current list provided by the Silver Springs Archives (subject to change):

Movies
1916: *The Seven Swans*   Richard Barthelmess, Marguerite Clark
1939: *Tarzan Finds A Son*   Jonnie Weissmuller, Maureen O'Sullivan
1946: *The Yearling*   Gregory Peck, Jane Wyman
1951: *Distant Drums*   Gary Cooper (Tommie Summers)
1954: *Creature from the Black Lagoon*   Richard Carlson, Julia Adams (Ricou Browning, Ginger Stanley)
1955: *Underwater*   Jane Russell, Richard Egan
1959: *Don't Give Up the Ship*   Jerry Lewis
1965: *Thunderball*   Sean Connery, Claudine Auger (underwater close-up shots)
1966: *Blindfold*   Rock Hudson, Claudia Cardinale
1979: *Moonraker*   Roger Moore (underwater fight with python)
1983: *Cross Creek*   Mary Steenburgen, Rip Torn
1983: *Never Say Never Again*   Sean Connery Kim Basinger
1985: *Legend*   Tom Cruise, Mia Sara, Tim Curry

TV
1958-1961: *Sea Hunt*—Lloyd Bridges (Episode: Girl in the Trunk)
1958: *The Arlene Francis Show*
1960s: *I Spy*   Robert Culp, Bill Cosby
1985: *One Life to Live*
1996: *Springs of North Florida* (National Geographic)
1999: *Crocodile Hunter* (Discovery Channel)   Steve Irwin
2002: *Ice Age Oasis* (BBC-TV Wild New World)

Commercials
1960s: Outboard Motor Commercial Mercury Motors
1980s: Silk Industry Commercial
1999: Crocodile Hunter   Steve Irwin
2001: Wrigley's Chewing Gum
2005: Coca Cola   (Mickie Summers)

Others
Unverified, with scenes possibly filmed at Silver Springs:

Movies
Land of Enchantment
1951: *Barefoot Mailman*   Robert Cummings, Terry Moore
1953: *Javiro*   Fernando Lamas, Arlene Dahl
1955: *Jupiter's Darling*   Esther Williams, Howard Keel
1955: *Rebel Without A Cause*   James Dean, Natalie Wood
1955: *Revenge of the Creature*   John Agar, Lori Nelson
1983: *Smokey and the Bandit 3*   Jackie Gleason, Burt Reynolds
2005: *Hoot*   Jimmy Buffet
2005: IMAX film—*Louisiana Wetlands*

TV Shows
1951-59: *You asked for It*
1960s: *The Jack Parr Show*
1960s: *Mutual of Omaha's Wild Kingdom*
1960s: *Make A Wish*
1960s: *Night Creatures* (National Geographic)
1970s: *Alien Animals of Florida*
1995: *Beyond 2000* (Discovery Channel)
1995: *Next Step* (Discovery Channel)
1994: *SeaQuest*   Roy Scheider
1979: *240 Robert*   Mark Harmon
1980s: *Rebel Lures*
1996: *Alligators & Crocodiles* (National Geographic)
1996: *Big Cypress Gator* (Discovery Channel)
1996: *Ultimate Guide to Crocodiles* (Discovery Channel)

Commercials
Waterproof Band-Aids (Johnson and Johnson)
Fishing Tackle (Dupont)
Financial Investments (Dean Witter)
(Note: Craig Littauer, Park Services Specialist, and the Silver Springs Archives crew are continuing to update and verify the current list.)

ABOUT THE AUTHOR

Dr. Robert Knight is the founder and director of the Howard T. Odum Florida Springs Institute, a nonprofit program dedicated to supporting science and education necessary for restoration and wise management of Florida's artesian springs. Dr. Knight is an environmental scientist with more than 38 years of professional experience in Florida, including detailed ecological studies at more than 20 large springs. He is former adjunct professor at the University of Florida Dept. of Environmental Engineering and Sciences where he taught graduate level classes on the ecology of Florida's springs and wetlands.

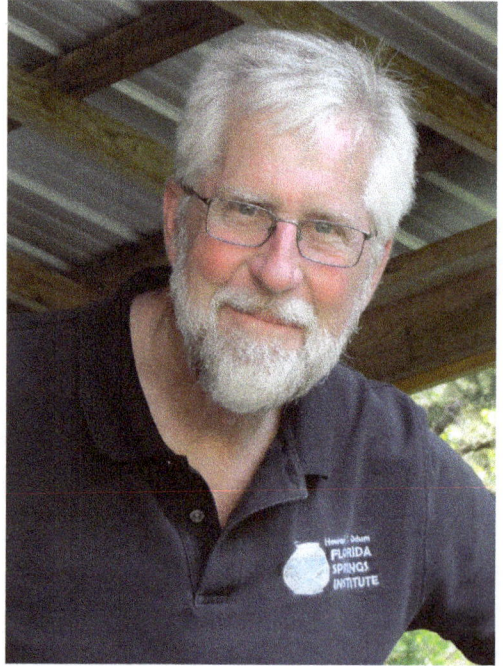

Dr. Robert L. Knight. Photo from author's personal collection, used by permission.

Follow Dr. Knight's work at the Florida Springs Institute.

ABOUT THE AUTHOR

Pulitzer Prize nominee for her work in the field of journalism, Marian Rizzo has won numerous awards, including the New York Times Chairman's Award and first place in the 2014 Amy Foundation Writing Awards. In addition to magazine writing, she worked for the Ocala Star-Banner Newspaper for 30 years, during which time she connected with local people from all walks of life and was drawn into the colorful tapestry of the area's environment.

Also an award-winning novelist, Marian lives in Ocala, Florida, with her daughter, Vicki, who has Down syndrome. Her other daughter, Joanna, has blessed her with three active grandchildren.

Pulitzer Prize nominee Marian Rizzo. Photo by Doug Engle Photography, used by permission.

ACKNOWLEDGEMENTS

With much appreciation we want to thank the *Ocala Star-Banner* for permission to reprint the articles and photos about people who worked at Silver Springs Attraction, and the *Gainesville Sun* for permission to reprint opinion pieces. Combined in one book, they create an historical treasure to be appreciated for many years to come.

Also, thanks go to Jennifer Hunt Murty, owner and publisher of *Ocala Style Magazine*, for granting permission to reprint the June 2020 story on photography legend, the late Bruce Mozert, titled "A Visionary Talent."

With great appreciation we thank the following springs friends and advocates for permission to reprint their texts and photos—Guy Marwick, Margaret Ross Tolbert, Rick Kilby, Rob Smith, and John Moran.

For assistance in converting the files for publication, thanks go to Jim Ross, managing editor and columnist at the *Ocala Star-Banner Newspaper,* and to Jen Cason, a friend and talented writer.

Many thanks also go to Photographic Archivist Adam Watson and his administrative assistant, Darrell Horton, for providing photos from the Bruce Mozert Collection and other collections in the Florida State Archives in Tallahassee.

Also our appreciation goes to Park Services Specialists, John Andrew "Andy" Kilmer and Craig Littauer, and the Silver Springs Archives crew for providing a list of films, TV shows, and commercials that were shot at Silver Springs Attraction.

Last, but not least, much gratitude goes to Mike Parker, publisher at WordCrafts Press, for taking on this enormous project and for bringing it to completion.

ALSO AVAILABLE FROM
WORDCRAFTS PRESS

Before History Dies
by Jacob M. Carter

A World War II Holiday Scrapbook
by Gail Kittleson & Cleo Lampos

Confounding the Wise
by Dan Kulp

Elders at the Gate
by Ray Blunt

Aerobics for the Mind
by Michael Potts, Ph.D.

www.wordcrafts.net

www.ingramcontent.com/pod-product-compliance
Lightning Source LLC
Chambersburg PA
CBHW080758300326
41914CB00055B/933